INtelLect WATCH

Watch your thoughts. Watch your reasoning.
Be strict with yourself.
Lay your own Standard, code of conduct, and
Adhere to it.

Ashwini Kumar Aggarwal

जय गुरुदेव

ISBN13: 978-81-952560-3-7 Paperback Edition
ISBN13: 978-81-952560-6-8 Hardbound Edition
ISBN13: 978-81-952560-5-1 Digital Edition

Title: Intellect Watch
Author: Ashwini Kumar Aggarwal

Printed and Published by
Devotees of Sri Sri Ravi Shankar Ashram
34 Sunny Enclave, Devigarh Road
Patiala 147001 Punjab, India

https://advaita56.weebly.com/
The Art of Living Centre

https://www.artofliving.org/

28th March 2021 Holi Full Moon, Phalguna Vasant Poornima

Chaitanya Mahaprabhu Jayanti, Lakshmi Jayanti, Vasant Ritu

Vikram Samvat 2077 Pramadi, Saka Era 1942 Sharvari.

From 29th March Chaitra Krishna Paksha begins, Hindu New Year, Vikram Samvat 2078 Ananda, whereas from 13th April Chaitra Shukla Paksha begins and change in Saka Samvat 1943 Plava.

1st Edition March 2021

जय गुरुदेव

Dedication

the most helpful, bountiful, supportive, graceful Master
H H Sri Sri Ravi Shankar

an offering at his lotus feet

Front Cover Image Credits

Juhi Bansal's calligraphy titled "Butterfly Mandala". Dated 7th October 2021

Preface

Intellect. Reason. Decision making. The ability to guide one's next thought, word or action.

Is it enhanceable?

Can we come to grips with our faculty to act? Can we shape it towards stable blissful human centric success?

This book is simply a collection of actual thoughts, possibly influencing my decisions, and an endeavor to cool the feverishness. It may or may not mirror yours. However, it has the potential to deflect or detach someone from sorrow, limitations, and rise up to reach for the stars by fulfilling their own vision.

WAVES of t h o u g h t s. Sense Feeling Emotion Memory Triggers.

S I N E W A V E S. Circles. SemiCircles. Tangents.

Whenever one dreams big, and follows it up with a degree of seriousness, something opens up deep within. It is what we call **"the *darshan* of the Presence"**.

CONTENTS

Snake Rope analogy

The Vedanta philosophy offers the following analogy to explain the state of a weak, terrified or ignorant mind.

You are walking along a dark pathway, on a lonely evening, and there is an uncertainty in your heart. Suddenly there is a slight noise amongst the bushes, a cool breeze tickles, and what looks like a slithering snake blocks your path a few meters ahead.

Now if your heart is stable, you might just continue without breaking step and upon coming close notice that the "thing" is immobile, and the idea "a twig or rope" might flash in your mind, and you continue walking over or by its side without faltering and the situation is past, no trace of any karma, no indelible impression on your mind.

On the other hand...
Why is this example quoted in Vedanta? What is the objective? Also consider Patanjali Yoga Sutra verse 1.6 Misconception, one of the five types of *vritti* thought waves, verse 1.30 the 9 *antaraya* Obstacles to attaining success, peace or joyous standing in life, verse 2.3 the 5 *klesha* Afflictions that manifest when obstacles are not solved nor surmounted.
It is the work of an entire lifetime to rise above the Snake Rope illusion. However, a short statement might work for the awakened: Do not entertain bitterness, do not allocate memory space to mistakes, mischiefs, the cruel or hurtful.
Again and again do the Advanced Meditation Course AMC
https://www.artofliving.org/in-en
https://www.artofliving.org/in-en/art-living-part-2-program
Jai Gurudev.

Blinkers for Horses

Or for me?
Certainly muffs for my ears.

Innocent or Not

Many a time i am clear at heart that how i see a situation is correct, healthy and visionary, however i do not communicate my viewpoint.

These are the times when i am NOT innocent. To put it more appropriately, this is how an "educated" "cultured" "responsible" individual behaves. It portrays a non-Innocent mind, that is totally different from guilty or wicked, at the same time that is lacking innocence.

<u>Then what is Innocence?</u>
Ponder, and come up with your own version.

Mine is a behavior that tarries not, not stopping to analyze, and simply puts in clear terms the heart's intent and viewpoint.

It is starkly evident in young children; it is what makes them adorable.

<u>Question</u>
In your life, has innocent behavior helped you more? Would you care to see more of that in society?

Me Myworld Lord Karma

Some say there are two of us, Me and the Lord.
Others opine there are three, Me, My Karma, and the Lord.
The enlightened of course say it is only one the Brahman.

My verdict is that there are 4 powerful entities that are always present in my life.

1. Me (the body and its needs, the mind and its desires)
2. My World (technically there is "one" universe in which we all exist; however my mind sees this universe from a particular angle, and that is my perception. It is my own superimposition on this creation, sort of like draping the universe in my own clothing. This is a big mystery, it is why i appear illogical to many, it is why the wise are rare and rarely understood) *Refer Bhagavad Gita verse 15.3*
3. Lord (an invisible yet tangible and powerful entity that we call by various names, Krishna, Guru, Durga, Brahman, Buddha, Shiva...) *Refer Bhagavad Gita verse 9.26*
4. Karma (a mystic principle that is the long-term debit-credit payload that transcends lifelines, that makes me behave in a polarized manner w.r.t some, that gives me talents or illnesses / failures or miracles that cannot be accounted for) *Refer Bhagavad Gita verse 4.17, 15.2*

न रूपमस्येह तथोपलभ्यते , नान्तो न चादिर् न च सम्प्रतिष्ठा ।

अश्वत्थमेनं सुविरूढमूलम् , असङ्गशस्त्रेण दृढेन छित्त्वा ॥ १५.३

na rūpamasyeha tathopalabhyate , nānto na cādir na ca sampratiṣṭhā | aśvatthamenaṁ suvirūḍhamūlam , asaṅgaśastreṇa dṛḍhena chittvā || 15.3 Bhagavad Gita

Just as the mind of a tree is stoic and incomprehensible, so is life's journey confusing. In a flash of bravery challenge the purpose and direction of life.

पत्रं पुष्पं फलं तोयम् ,   यो मे भक्त्या प्रयच्छति ।

तद् अहं भक्त्युपहृतम् , अश्नामि प्रयतात्मनः ॥ ९.२६

patraṁ puṣpaṁ phalaṁ toyam , yo me bhaktyā prayacchati | tad ahaṁ bhaktyupahṛtam , aśnāmi prayatātmanaḥ || 9.26 BG

Whether thee be an illiterate villager, or a skilled artisan, or a highly accomplished and cultured personality, all qualify to attain Divine union since a pure heart is the only permit. Leaf-flower-fruit is an oft quoted simile for the buffoon-mediocre-intelligent.

कर्मणो ह्यपि बोद्धव्यम् , बोद्धव्यं च विकर्मणः ।

अकर्मणश्च बोद्धव्यम् , गहना कर्मणो गतिः ॥ ४.१७

karmaṇo hyapi boddhavyam,boddhavyaṁ ca vikarmaṇaḥ |

akarmaṇaśca boddhavyam , gahanā karmaṇo gatiḥ || 4.17 BG

A fine intellect is needed to discriminate between right and wrong, since situations present themselves such that what was correct in the first becomes inappropriate in the next. Unpredictable, nay unfathomable are the events across time.

अधश् चोर्ध्वं प्रसृतास् तस्य शाखाः , गुणप्रवृद्धा विषयप्रवालाः ।

अधश्च मूलान्यनुसन्ततानि , कर्मानुबन्धीनि मनुष्यलोके ॥ १५.२

adhaś cordhvaṁ prasṛtās tasya śākhāḥ , guṇapravṛddhā viṣayapravālāḥ | adhaśca mūlānyanusantatāni , karmānubandhīni manuṣyaloke || 15.2 Bhagavad Gita

Majestic branches spread all around are like the virtues and vices strengthened by alert senses. Firm roots anchor the tree just as great deeds make a man well entrenched in life.

What Works

Many a time students and lay folk have queried:
please tell the formula for qualitative and quantitative change...
please elaborate how may we do better...
is there a way to achieve big targets?

Age old wisdom has stated time and again
- i n t e n s e Passion

- s i n c e r e Effort

- c h e e r f u l Patience

- l o t s of Time

Refer Patanjali Yoga Sutra verse 1.14

Notes

स तु दीर्घकालनैरन्तर्यसत्कारासेवितो दृढभूमिः । 1.14 Patanjali Yoga Sutra

sa tu dīrghakālanairantaryasatkārāsevito dṛḍhabhūmiḥ ।

1.14 And that when continuous over a long period of time with sincere devotion, establishes firm foundation.
Our life gets the benefit of Abhyaasa only in due course of time. Our temperament becomes firm only after many years of practice. The yogic foundations become strongly rooted in our consciousness only after prolonged habit. That too when our practice is full of Sincerity and when our heart is filled with Devotion.

What comes a Cropper

Continuing from the above, many have been surprised that their efforts did not yield the desired fruit. What doesn't work or what is the cause for failure in umpteen cases:

- great Talent

- lots of Money

- undue Cleverness

Yukti Bhakti Shakti Mukti

We look at the previous discussion through the eyes of the Master. Guruji says we need to apply yukti bhakti shakti mukti, all the four together.

- Bhakti as the main course PASSION

- Shakti as the regular discipline EFFORT

- Yukti as an appropriate pinch of salt S O M E T I M E S

- Mukti as faith that Lord has heard, shall process TIMELY

Enormity of Creation

This creation is v a s t. It is enormous. There is space for all and any thoughts, emotions, energies, forces, particles.

Sometimes it appears one is left out. That is momentary. At times one feels luckless, that too is soon changed.

Remember that this CREATION is ENORMOUS. It has the potential for anything to manifest. There is the possibility for the greatest to become extinct.

Each one of us, whether man or beast or gadget or principle, is WELCOME here.

No matter what one's ideology, what one's temperament, what one's proclivity, what one's weakness, what one's generosity, there is space and a time for one's presence and function.

The angle of perception, and the point of reference is fluid. It is reconfigurable.

It accommodates the cruelest will and the most dangerous of energies. It rewards the smallest action and erases the biggest phenomenon. It nurtures and protects each fiber, each cell, each fraction and each construct. It is the playground for the coarsest of tongues and the magnificent of munificence's.

Lord's Love

1035am 9.10.2021
Bhagvati Sundari, how is catramide eye drops?
1107am Its very nice. I am using. Eyes are burning.

1206am 8.10.2021
Mummy ji how do you do? Am missing you

658pm 6.10.2021
Flame meets Lord at noon on Tuesday 5.10.2021. Chats gaily
recounts the whole episode beginning with Guruji's Soudhamini
visit at 9pm on 2.10.2021. Jumping up and down as she's been
crowned big mom. "Founder of Herbs and Herbal Medicines", to set
up new venture from scratch.

216pm 6.10.2021
Form talks fond love recalling the early days.

110pm 5.10.2021
Fabulous 4 meeting W M J J over coffee.

1134am 5.10.2021
Consort and Victory joyous chat with, during fortune filled drive
Ludhiana to Patiala.

927am 5.10.2021
How are things? How is the yoga book coming up?
931am Things are good mammu. I am working on the book. Have
written 10 pages, will finish the written part and then start placing
the pictures.

1046am 29.9.2021
Started for Rishikesh. Happy Time. Tata
1054am Wish you happy journey. Happy time!

411am 3.10.2021
Aapki yaad aati hai. Kisi din hamara project hoga Ganga jitna long Rishikesh se Sunderbans...
218pm 3.10.2021 Dearie called and happily said - O so we shall stay together?

451pm 26.9.2021
A wonderfully depicted book. No one can think that a negative human nature like greed can be seen in a positive light-------it says GREED should be directed towards creative works or preserving natural beauty.

Another seemingly negative word-----Intoxicants-----if you wish to be intoxicated, immerse in devotional singing. Wah kya baat hai. C

430am 26.9.2021
Snow awakened me, brought a jugful of homemade milk with dates, Fineness ate to her heart's content.

836am 22.09.2021
Yaar aap call hi nahin karti. Naaraj ho???
932am 25.9.2021 Ice called and kept on talking until she came close and touched. "I returned last night so first thing I called you this morning, now you can talk anytime as I am alone at home."

407am 16.09.2021
J's coronation. Shukla Paksha Dashami.

907-1003am 15.09.2021
Guru Puja Havan

1048am 14.09.2021
Saw your message just now. Sorry for having missed it. Thanks for

your good wishes. Where are you? We are in Pune these days. Any possibility of your coming this side in near future. With love and blessings. ik
1133am Lots of Love. Shall be seeing you Soon
416pm 16.9.2021 Love to meet you.

249am 14.09.2021
Dear Rain, on selfish's birthday ensure that she is dressed in a teenage outfit, give her a tight Hug and Kiss, make her feel young, wanted, loved. Tell her she's a great girl and her life can become a shining example.
829am Many thanks 🖤 dear. Her Birthday is on 24th but shall convey your warm wishes to her. Thanks so much for remembering. Wishing you loads of health and good luck.

10-1133am 11.09.2021
Lotus Girl speaks excitedly non-stop. Like a baby who has finally found love.

738am 10.09.2021
Kal busy thi isliye phone nhi ho paya. Kaise hai aap?
841am Devi aaj Ganesh puja mein aapke darshan huai. Ji you are fantastic. Ganesha always protects you.

808am 14.09.2021
Ji just reached at Kolhapur home.

1108pm 9.09.2021
I got courier today. Sorry couldn't call you. Thank you so much dear.
334am Devi aap ki beauty aparam par hai. You are the most perfect girl whose divinity is of the highest order. I touch your holy feet.

836am 8.09.2021
I really enjoyed your presence here, maybe you got bored.........I'm lucky you did Rudra Abhishek at my house.
420pm Wow. Mummy Papa really feel great on meeting you.
434pm I am very happy to have them with me on my special day.

959am 7.09.2021
Excited Bharya chats bubbling joyfully.

437pm 7.09.2021
You will find synergist brochure right at the end of this article
nbnawithnee

930pm 6.09.2021
India wins. Thank You Lord Sri Sri Ravi Shankar.

1105pm 5.09.2021
Precious teacher 🖤 Happy Teachers Day.
1107pm Yes dear 🖤 Happy Teacher's Day to you too. K

939am 5.09.2021
a Teacher is a Precious Wealth and pillar of Society. Happy
Teachers Day.

698pm Thank you too much dear child. You are our precious
student...when r u coming home?
940am Thanku so much bhaiya. And same high blessings for you.
Delicate

1006am Resp. Dear Ashwani ji, Shikshak diwas par aapko bhi
dheron shubh kaamnayen! Each one of us do and can TEACH (Life
lessons) to many many from our actions, intentions and deeds!!
Celebrate being a TEACHER! Kind regards Prayers and blessings.
Limited n Bound

933am
Pranaams Mataji, a Teacher is a Precious Wealth and pillar of
Society. Happy Teachers Day. Jai Gurudev
115pm Thank you Ashwini. All love and best wishes

319pm Thanks and same to you dear 🖤 Pleasure Bharya
708pm Happy teacher's day Swamiji 🖤 Golden

224pm 4.09.2021
Today I got another courier in which eye drops are there… i was
very angry and wanted to scold you earlier…
458pm Honey dew drop hugged me tight, held hands and kissed.

1059am 4.09.2021
Looking forward to your visit. Regards. Amritsar

2.09.2021
Today I walked out of prison. Feel the freedom. Thank you, Bhaiya.

658pm 1.09.2021
Synergist - Let us kindle the fire within, have you met yours yet? Met
Lord at 1240pm in Ganga on 8.8.21

1113am 31.08.2021
Golden's paper published in prestigious journal and PhD bagged.

1028am 31.08.2021
Mummy ji may i visit you
1032am Yes dear…do come

756pm 30.08.2021
Dearie sat next to me holding my hands and cooed loving sounds,
feeling totally free and at ease, her fragrance was sweet her skin
soft.

909am Janmashtami
Radha ko Janmashtami ka dher sara pyar
1120am Aapko bhi bhaut bhaut shubhkaamanayeee… Kaise hai aap?

1227am 27.8.2021
Thanks bhaiya for sparing your valuable time for the visit. You will
be happy to hear that I will be joining the advance course from 28-
30 Aug
654am O wow Janmashtami special. That is what makes you so
divine and adorable. All the best for Guru Grace Protection and
Prosperity.

958am 25.08.21
For fruit   to ripen, intense effort and lots of time are the
ingredients. Money or cleverness have no role since the nectar gets
made in the divine realm.

1016pm 24.08.2021
Thank you so much. Bharya Humility
1020pm 26.08.2021 Mummy and Papa are heavenly. They served
me the tastiest dinner and gave me enormous blessings. Thank You

728pm 23.08.2021
Troy is Bodh Gaya ashram incharge and brimming with confidence,
responsibility and productivity.

1108am 10.08.2021
Your OTP to register/access CoWIN is 505685. It will be valid for 3
minutes. CoWIN

1113am 10.08.2021
Congratulations! You have successfully completed the schedule of
all doses of COVID-19 vaccine. You can download your certificate at
https://cowin.gov.in

945-10pm 8.8.2021 Amavasya
Beloved sang romantic songs. Fondly kissed and held tight.
Thrilling and so Joyous. Full of cheerfulness.

Your Presence

8 Days basti is a good way to detox, slim down, feel energetic all day. Flame

Wake up 4am said Lord on Thursday 5.8.2021 8:30pm thru PK.

1206pm 7.8.2021 Bangalore Airport
Bharya Adoration joyous as Lovefilled married, Littleflow ki sagai.

1214pm 7.8.2021
A happy dancing Consort. Wah.

955pm 7.8.2021
Mummy ji the rains and rainbow are making life sweet, love you

1008am 7.8.2021
Darshan of Lord in the form of blissful Golden, 9am trustee Stiffshape at Shivalaya.

1212pm 6.8.2021
Shower of blessings from Rishiji, who enumerated Yoga Vasishta, and said I was keeping my senses under control and living a disciplined yogic life.

Nariyal pani delicious ashram kitchen gate milk booth.

1110pm 6.8.2021
Midnight at Soudhamini. Amazing mechanical mobile tripod.

1031am 6.8.2021
Called PatialaMind and he happily shared that I came in his dream yesterday morning at the time Lord made me his.

8pm 6.8.2021
Flame announces noq-21 100% effective, tested at Frankfurt.
Pancreas shaped ♡ leaf seen in Chandragiri Forest Tamil Nadu.
Surest cure for diabetes. VLord is proud with excellent HCL new job,
laptop, showers of Guru grace.

651pm 6.8.2021
Jai Gurudev am at bullandpuri Gurudwara Sahib right now. The
place we visited with architect, feeling blessed to have your call.

301pm 6.8.2021
Royal lunch at Lord's kitchen followed by scooter ride and dessert
at Amruth restaurant at Panchakarma. Laughter with plumber and
poison.

1019am 6.8.2021
Such a delightful girl delicate, says she has so much grace and love
and support of Guruji.

805pm 5.8.2021
C welcomes Rudra Puja.

830pm 5.8.2021
Intuition process for adults by Lord. 20 initiated including tired
commander, brittle peacock, and others. Secretary mammoth
wakes up at 3am (regularly?) to take 90min yoga.

551pm 5.8.2021
Honey dew drop kissed and hugged tight, her fragrance spilling
over, her proximity elevating, for 18min.
5.8.2021
1246pm R our ashram electrician gives a cord. Thank You my Lord.
1pm Sickly cowering finance desk. Devyawn front.
1216pm kotdwar call while at Sumeru Travels for chennai booking.
904am Shiva inspires from Benign Earth.
941am Prateek swami training at Shivalaya, Sambasadashiva
temple consecrated on 20th July 2020.

1113am PnP of Guru Puja training, showered so much blessings.
They use my books.

1033am 5.8.2021
With Lord, at his feet, in total samarpan. Mind still, heart tranquil,
body fit. Sri Sri School of Yoga for 40 minutes.
Tithi dvadashi pradosh vrat, Wednesday day of Sri Krishna, Ardra
nakshatra. ssrvm trustees photoshoot and talk by Gurudev.

Lord turns and looks deeply inside ♥ my eyes, his right hand gives
a playful powerful message for uplifting Sanskrit. Making our
University and reinventing Education.

925am 4.8.2021
Dear Radha, am visiting Bangalore Ashram for Guruji's Grace and
Love. Jai Gurudev.

1018pm 3.8.2021
Is entry to Ashram allowed now. How was the flight?
1019pm
Yes Papa. Excellent.

1119pm 3.8.2021
Dear Aggarwal, Please visit clps.co/X8tvi9aqv for report. Thanks,
GMC Patiala, at Civil Hospital Ludhiana.

525pm 29.7.2021
Chatted with a happy darling. Radha aaj khush ho kar gheri neend
lena. Sweet Dreams. Blissful Sleep.

640am 27.7.2021
Dear Aggarwal, Your vaccination for 2nd dose is due 30-07-2021.
Please schedule your appointment on cowin.gov.in.

710am 25.7.2021
Rose fragrance during live meditation by Guruji.

7pm
Lord gave me a blissful divine healing and strengthening Rudra
Puja evening at MnM. Thank You Shiva.

510am 24.7.2021
Jupiter hung like a big diamond, the moon was orange, faint
behind a cloud cover setting to the west.

The 5 Points

- Wake up early, bath, comb
- Continue the Sanskrit books
- Continue GuruPuja Havan
- Long Walks and Singing
- Clean bathrooms

330pm rose fragrance during hollow and empty. Online AMC.

Arrived in my own Realm

1030pm 22.7.2021

I went out unable to sleep.

It was like entering into another world, the world of my choice.

All the lights were on, shining brightly, there was happy chatter from neighbor's family, and the stars shone glistening.

Jupiter was bigger than Venus, and so close, the moon lit the sky with its silvery glow.

It felt as if I had arrived in the place I had always yearned for.

8pm 21.7.2021

Lo and behold, Rudra Puja time got changed to evening as I had wished...

648am 20.7.2021

A pleasant nourishing rain with thick cloud cover, I waited for a couple of minutes, suddenly the sun shone. He came specially to greet me, no physics could explain it, just the Lord's tight presence.

712am 19.7.2021

Radha aaj mausam bahut pyar bhara hai. Cool breeze and drizzle. Good Morning 🖤

944am Very good morning. Have a lovely day

1004am Thanks very much Tripura Sundari

You can do Anything

5pm 19.7.2021
Lord said - you can actually do anything, just be on the path.

8pm 16.7.2021
Guruji said all's well. I'm in charge. Everything's taken care of. Live free. Live joyously.

127am 15.7.2021

Rain Dear, how's your birthday? Did you find what you wanted - Love Compassion Forgiveness and Pleasure???

749am Thanks Ashwini!! I'd a good time tenth ♥ God is kind ... thanks for your blessings as always.

1052pm 14.7.2021

Devi aap khush ho na? Sweet dreams.

1205am Ji... Thodi busy hun aaj kal. Mummy papa aaye hue hain. Guest bhi hain.

127am Ok Radha. Take Care. All the best. Bahut yaad aa rahi hai

129am Kyu. Take care.

8am 14.7.2021

Lord Sri Krishna said - I'm right here with you. Drop all anxiety. Monsoon Rainfall abundance, peace, bliss.

8pm 14.7.2021

The sky is very beautiful right now. It's a perfect day

802pm wow. C

954pm 4.7.2021

Today I went through the picture-perfect book that you published recently. Its amazing piece of creativity invested life time memories. I had to leave early today. Wish to sit with you sometime, Kind regards. Limited nBound

654am 5.7.2021 Wow Goddess Lakshmi. Thee have the spark to bring out the best. Happy Time and All the Best. Jai Gurudev

912am Waao... Jai Gurudev your words are so encouraging, your works are so enriching... you are indeed amazing Ashwani ji ... Wish you HIS grace !!

1124am 3.7.2021

Baby's call is right on time as I get covaxin jab.

1123am Mohali Civil Hospital

Your OTP to register/access CoWIN is 707588.

You have successfully been vaccinated with your 1st Dose with COVAXIN on 03-07-2021 at 11:24 AM. You may download your vaccination Certificate from https://cowin.gov.in

723am 3.7.2021

Devi I am going to get vaccine. Please bless me

826am All the best. God bless you dear. Ishwar's divinity is always with you forever.

217pm Jai Gurudev Radha. Ji today you have given me full protection. I am feeling your presence and love. It makes me feel very safe and happy. Thanks very much Devi.

6am 2.7.2021

Morning Padmasadhana. Body said I'm absolutely fit.

12noon 1.7.2021

Rudra Puja with delicacy. Resounding success as at 515pm Mummy waves me a cheerful bye.

8am 1.7.2021

Bhaiya said - I am here - drop all reservation, agitation, flicker

6am 2.7.2021

Felt fit while doing padmasadhana. Wow Shiva.

509am 1.7.2021

Dear Ashwini....

Wishing you many many happy returns of the day (a bit belated though).... God bless you with abundance of good health and unlimited happiness....Assam

846am Thanks a ton dear. Your words ring true and touch the heart. Makes me feel so pleased and joyous.

God is Mine

12midnight 30.6.2021
Mummy teaches Manju dussar and all have a terrific game.

10pm Mummy Papa sing happily, radiating joy, all join in.
9pm Cake cutting with ahãnā

546pm 30.6.2021
Rain cooes all love.

30.6.2021
410pm Happy birthday mont, best wishes and lots of love and blessings. Git
421pm Thanks, it's a great season of success for all.

535pm Happy birthday to dear Ashwini. Soudhamini 2nd floor
554pm Thanks. Your wishes make me feel splendid

1037am
Shiva from ashram chats happily, bestows Lord's grace.

10am 28.6.2021
Baby dissolves in love.

7pm 28.6.2021
Lord and bharya MorningDew Rudra Puja infinite grace.

6am 26.6.2021
Had darshan of Lord, he disconnected my bondages, absorbed me within a pool of bliss. Magic to unfold through the day and beyond.

5pm 25.6.2021
Felt physically fit and relaxed sitting at the tube well farm 5.6 km away. J says he's gone through a DSN.

756pm 25.6.2021
Honey dew drop happily chatted, as we ate together and dissolved in each other. Her thick scent is overpowering.

8pm 24.6.2021

- Dialogue with soft spoken bullandpuri Maharaj.

- Meteor Shower. Full Moon.

- Brightness of a Boy in our architect.

- Baby Bday Cake.

430am 23.6.2021
Guru Puja Havan new complex

103pm 21.6.21
979656 is OTP at RIDHA.

Such a solidified Brahman consciousness. Such Guru Grace, belongingness and acceptance.

Such a tranquil, collected, silent mind. Thank You Shiva.

Thanks for a soulful rendering of Japji Sahib at 230pm.

Thanks for a children's get together at 430pm.

856am 21.6.21
Tripura Sundari, today is International Day of Yoga. Please give half hour to Yoga and Meditation ji

10am Yes ji. I did it. Reached vishwamitri...
1005am Lovely. Ji you are a perfect goddess

919pm 16.6.2021
Radha calls her voice golden and full of joy.

751am 21.6.21
Jai Gurudev sir I will reach nearby 12:15 noon today
840am Wonderful. It's a most happy and divine day

826pm 16.6.2021
J's J says she's had a fabulous 2 months.

1142am 16.6.2021
J calls to update that things are back on track with renewed
enthusiasm and mighty successful.

717am 16.6.2021
Honey dew drop says she missed me so much these past 10 days,
so an outpouring of sweet love.

11.6.2021
snow maiden makes love, this time kissing and holding tight.

10.6.2021
Amazing that mistress remembers our sweet love-making.

6.6.2021
kdp shows sale of 18 books, largest in single day so far. Also, Sandhi
Handbook is at no 3 in Phonics Bestsellers.

850pm 4.6.2021
No please don't do that... Anyway, I am going to mother's place, I
will watch there.....
854pm Have a wonderful holiday and enjoy lots. Good Night Sweet
Dreams
855pm Thanks

3.6.2021 1230pm to 930pm
A joy-filled healing drive to Bathinda with Mummy Papa in orange skoda.

8pm 31.5.2021 & 4pm 1.6.21
Our white flowers Tree bid adieu in a thunderstorm. Then next day when the gardener came, it joyously got freed of its roots and transcended to the plane of eternal grace. Jai Gurudev Shiva. Thanks Guruji for resolving all the issues amicably and making us resilient and resourceful and renewed during AMC.

5am 30.5.2021
Peacocks heard when I looked out of the main door to see if Venus was there.

840pm 28.5.2021
Free chat with a happy and relaxed J.

912am 25.5.2021
Dear A, many thanks for the Vedic Nasal Drops. It is revolutionary since it shall prevent all respiratory ailments, improve eyesight, promote sound sleep and improve digestion when applied in nabhi.

6pm 24.5.2021
Flocks and droves and an abundance of 56 number plates, as my Lord signaled my freedom and rejoiced.

9am 23.5.2021
Received nectar from Lord sitting on park bench, felt the dimension of abundance.

140pm 21.5.21
She made love, full of romance and amorous playfulness.

12noon 21.5.21
Had a profound feeling of being healed and taken care of. Deep Meditation. In the morning sandstone took me to show the three sitting on charpoy, and as we watched mano came to say morning. She happily related their moods and their strong affinity.

Earlier at 5am it rained, and the outpouring was full of love, the winds were caressing, the raindrops were actually nectar, and as I sipped them, a freedom washed over me.

803am 21.5.21
Namaste ji. Yashoda attained final liberation at 6:30pm yesterday evening. Jai Gurudev
756pm Namaste ji. Yashoda Amma was a soft and elevated person apart from being a writer poet in both Tamil and Telugu. Praying for her higher 'gati' on her onward journey.

Thank you for sharing news about a dearly known higher soul. V

802pm Yes Ashwini salutations to the departed soul. Mataji

1132am 20.5.2021
Yes ji I was remembering yesterday only

9am 16.5.2021
Today I ascend to another plane having satiated caressing rain n unduly selfish. Thus, I qualify for the benevolence epitomized by snow.

14.5.2021 Akshay Tritiya
7am Morning heard Peacock.

908am Baby Beauty laughing said she's having guests for lunch, and said emphatically she shares her password only with me.

1004am Consort is having white pumpkin juice and consulting with acupuncture specialist sharma.
1244pm Jee felt a load taken off his head and totally at ease.
621pm Golden confirms that our University shall soon be operational.

13.5.2021 Birthday
Light Drizzle, Cool Weather, Warm, Hot, Windy, all five seasons experienced.

823pm 12.5.2021
Jgd Swamy ji. Yes, we will join. 🖤 Youthful

908am 12.5.2021
Am sure uncle & aunty are great. Happy Tera Mai Guruji's Birthday
349pm Yes ji both are well. Thanks for your wishes. Rani Jhansi Road.

11.5.2021
1230pm for an unknown reason she laughed carefree.
3pm our own Yoga book now nears completion.
4pm Jee called to say Vidow was cured.
830pm a report that LimitnBound was being released.
9pm Kailash Kalimpong finally got awakened.
6am all of it in a dream stating that these were simple engineering sums.

834am 11.5.2021
Devi we are busy with making chappan bhog for Guruji's birthday on 13 May. If you wish we can do Yoga and Chanting and Meditation together and eat Kheer at 2pm on 13th. Jai Gurudev
947am OK 🖤 have a nice time and enjoy the auspicious event.

1258pm 9.5.2021
Katti with her. Thank you Guruji.
1251pm Radha aaj kya khilaogi?
1253pm Dal rice.

1135am 8.5.2021
Good to have you as co-participant in Sahaj. Ha!
1224pm Oh you also attended! :) VLord

830pm 7.5.2021
Dishu gave Mummy Papa a superb half hour, showing Muktsar visit
village photos and chatting and all enjoyed thoroughly and felt
light and strong.

1118pm 6.5.2021
Today weather is cool and like hill station, remembering you too
much. Sweet dreams

1040am 4.5.21
J calls happy and brimming with success.

1230pm 3.5.2021
Baby called unexpectedly, nectar dripping voice, pregnant with
desire.

819pm 1.5.2021
Dearie called in the mood for love, sounding fresh, fit and amorous.

6am Morning we had a delicious breakfast and were soon blessed

by large raindrops.

701pm 29.4.2021

Golden called for wedding invite

1020am 30.4.2021 Wishing a Wedding of love peace and joy that lays the foundation of a great University for evolution and emancipation of mankind.

28.4.2021

Git gets jab. First in Family.

7am 28.4.2021

caressing rain you are family and very well taken care of.

1006am Thanks so much Stay blessed always

27.4.2021 Chaitra Poonam

Lord conducts live Meditation after 2 months. Pothi reports 22 print books sale, biggest in single day so far.

906am 24.4.2021

Radha last night you gave me lots of bliss. Through the night I kept remembering you and your sweet voice, and your thick fragrance filled me.

1230pm Dearie called to make love on divine plane.

901pm 23.4.2021

Honey dew drop came and started to kiss, she enjoyed being caressed. One of the most blissful heavenly times we spent together.

732pm 23.4.21

Gurudev we got license for plaza today. Will start work from Monday onwards. We seek your blessings for completion of this project on time. 814pm Jai Gurudev. Great News and stupendous efforts by yourself and your team. It shall be the Pride of Punjab.

Om Namah Shivaya

J called to say our new city would be built, the sankalpa had been made.

8pm 20.4.21
Did Havan and all's well. Inhaler works like a charm.
940pm Ok thanks Mont

120pm 19.4.2021
Thanks Flame. It cures within 2 days of proper use
355pm Nice Bhaiya, so happy to know, have done the purchase

1217pm
Good. Shall get it . Thanks a lot for your Suggestion.
Jayanti n bhai

Noon 18.4.2021
News of an Earth-shattering discovery. Lord has finally made sister boss over all the governments and big business on the planet.

Guruji becomes first citizen of planet Earth. Doors to intergalactic travel open and mankind's efforts bear success.

1056pm 16.4.2021
Slept in Snow in a tight hug, her lips oozing nectar, her kissing icefull, legs fused.

Had always wished that I could be at Absolute zero. Now I was.

531pm 16.4.2021
Today the storm came and our drumstick tree fell down
Exactly 2 years and 20 feet tall, with a trident ♥ stem.

628pm Okay, mammu. Glad everyone is safe.
7pm Yes a great blessing it bestowed on all, it came to participate in our home making and once it was sure the Lord had been infused and properly stationed, and a good fortune was beginning to unfold, it left for the milky way galaxy.

433pm 13.4.2021 Baisakhi
Baby Beauty made love as she was all alone by herself on the express to vishwamitri.

111pm 13.4.2021 Baisakhi
J called and his voice had a deep peace and cheeriness.

733am 12.3.21 Sompati Masya
An illness is very temporary and is a great time to realize what a fortunate existence we have.
838am Yes. I have that realization. C

556pm 30.3.2021
Wanted to share good news - with your blessings, daughter got Surgery Residency at Mayo Clinic, which ranks at Number 1 in hospitals of USA and World 🖤
622pm Om Namah Shivaya. Superb efforts.

718pm 29.3.2021
Happy Holi
856pm Brilliant. Thanks very much Rainy Shiny

630pm 23.3.2021
Saw J Bairstow batting. He looks like you.
328pm 24.3.2021 Monty you are lucky and God sent. Sonu

410pm 20.3.2021
Well how about telling me after listening to my experience. Consort
746am 21.3.2021 You are Stunning. You are Superb. You are a Super
Woman. 925am 💜 Thank you so much. It's so nice of you to say so.
God bless you 💜

909pm 16.3.21
" Om Svasti". Jai Gurudev, read your book " Gheranda Samhita".
It's very deep, needs a lot of discussion with you to know many new
secrets of spirituality. But this time higher level of perfection is felt.
Gurudev, I congratulate you for this masterpiece. Feeling blessed to
have this book in my hands.
1005am 17.3.21 Thanks ji for your appreciation. Makes me Happy.
1007am Your presence in our life is real blessing for all of us.

15-18th Mar 2021
A happiness course gifted by the great Lord. Took a lot of load off
my shoulders, made me feel alive and rejuvenated.
Registered 17 except for GSing. 18 participants attended.

1018pm 11.3.21
You are loved and you are lovely, Om Namah Shivaya
1042pm So are you Dear. JGD daman
1228am Thanks dear & Same wish for you. Pleasure Bharya
201am Hello bhaiya, thank you for your message and loving wishes
on Mahashivratri :)
939am Dear Ashwini Bhaiya. Jai Gurudev. Thanks for your best
wishes. Wish you happy Shivaratri. Ayurveda

433pm 10.3.21
Bhagavati Devi ko Shivaratri ki purnatvam
631pm Tumhe bhi.

1051am 8.3.21
Had darshan of smiling Lotus girl at Dandiswami, she was oozing oomph, looking absolutely fit, cheerful, with attractive eyes.

8-930am Lord came in the form of pedicure and manicure, somehow he made me feel that I would make it to the Divine plane this Shivratri.

112pm 7.3.21
Sri, mailed shabad - re man aeso kar sanyasa, and it's English.
1016am 8.3.21 A conduct pure and calm indicating you are content. You are marvelous Jee

9.18pm 4.3.2021
Good Night Radha. Sweet Dreams
936pm Good night
23rd Feb vaDelhiLucknow
4th Mar return lkn-blr-va, great darshan of Ram Mandir on 2nd March and Hanuman.

542am 28.2.21
Happy Birthday Dishu. I understand you sense this life is Divine and can be lived brilliantly. Go ahead and achieve the same.
1104am Thank You so much Mammu! I am going to achieve this.

826am 26.2.21
Jupiter in 8th house also describes your personality better Sri :)
The individual may get financial help and back-up from family, relatives, friends and society at large. Native is highly intuitive, intellectual, compassionate, sensual, emotional, and sensitive. These natives should use their energies positively to empower humanity and serve mankind. Their sole purpose in life should be

to help the highly fortunate or creative or genuine folk.
828am It's grace alone that showers from you Jee
920am Sri, astrology to this extent is truly guiding light...

1021pm 24.2.21
Radha hope you reached Lucknow and are comfortable and happy
1022pm Yes... Reached safely. Yesterday I called two times but you
didn't receive...
922am Happy Time Devi. You are Beautiful Strong Divine and
Successful

238pm 16.2.21
Happy Basant Panchami & Saraswati Puja!!!! Caressing rains
7pm Thanks 🖤

401pm 14.2.21
Tripura Sundari ko valentine day ka pyaar pranaam aur charan
sparsh
421pm Apko bhi happy valentine's day

1044pm 12.2.21
I called you 2-3 times, when I went for bank work. I wanted your ac
no. But your phone was switched off.
1045pm Radha I had gone for puja and havan
1058pm OK

702am 13.2.2021
Now tomorrow I am going to Nareshwar and from there, Somnath
jyotirling. After one week will come back.
703am How is your Russell Hobbs?
704am Yes, it's nice and comfortable.

1256pm 13.2.2021
Devi you are too beautiful and Divine. Aapke charan sparsh. Jai
Gurudev

630pm 12.2.21
Got the grace of meeting a soft-spoken Sanskrit teacher.
1230pm got to press bharya's feet and she felt blissful. Thank You
Bhaiya. Jai Gurudev

2pm 11.2.21
met my darling Morning Dew. Felt the grace and attention shower
of Lord.

955pm 11.2.21
Received Hatha Ratnavali by M.L Gharote
1056pm Wow. Hope you like it
1248pm 12.2.21 The text is clear, and all asanas pictures are
shown...it is a good book mammu.

4pm 10.2.21
During reading of Garud Puran heard in the 16th chapter that
Breath in is So and exhale is Hum.

8.2.21
Jai Guru Dev.
Want to talk to you, when can I call you ?
Lots and Lots of Love and Regards. Vidhya
1133pm
Wow. What a pleasant surprise. Charan Sparsh. Jai Gurudev

5pm to 10pm 7.2.2021
Lord came for knowledge session in the form of Guna with a tight
group of 25. In fact, all seats got filled quickly. Stayed for dinner and
then went to bed!!! Ye

1230pm 5.2.21
Mummy Papa reached fine. You are perfect in taking good care.

1231pm Thanks a lot. Pleased Bharya.
1232pm Welcome home back from Ludhiana. Mummy in great form.

Morning 4.2.21
Felt healed during morning Sadhana, completely at last.

Also had a wonderful feeling from last night's dream, wherein a celestial lass spent some minutes talking to me, then in the end kissed me and we become one.

1233pm 3.2.21
S'vati related an amazing experience of Lord at Kamalashile with her son on Monday 4th and Tuesday 5th Jan. Guruji arrived at 9pm on 4th and did Durga Homa on 5th morning before driving to Kollur Mukambika temple where her AMC teacher welcomed Him.

10am 2.2.21
Papa Mummy leave for Ludhiana, smartly dressed and cheerful. Jai Gurudev Shiva.

1.2.21
today too experienced deep healing meditation afternoon.

31.1.21
noon meditation
Was too deep, went into trance after a long time.

530pm 30.1.21
A bright and cheery and happy call from dearie full of high spirits. Returned from Amreli Ayurveda today after nadi panchakarma and feeling so good after stay of 13 days.

1020am 30.1.21
A most noble and significant milestone achieved. Personal Sadhana
is the hub on which the foundation of greatness rests
1022am Thanks Gurudev. All because of your support

730pm 29.1.21
J calls to say he has today completed 12 years of morning Sadhana,
a sankalpa he took and followed with determination.

708pm 28.1.21
Golden happily calls to say engagement on 25th April, marriage on
30th April.

28.1.21
Papa related dream he had of basic course being conducted on
terrace of Mali Ganj home with Guruji, and he and Guruji sitting on
an empty jute bag used as a mattress.

28.1.21
Poornima received DCard
6:18pm Validated and deposited cash by Git

1048am 26.1.21
sms got 1232 24427 04:57:16

716pm 10.1.21
Happy 2021...! Kindly share in your group and do register yourself
too... ♥ aolt.in/529784 Online iExcel Holistic Well Being Program
14-17 Jan 2021, 7-9am. Special session with Gurudev on 17th
1130am sms received as Lord beckons.
737am 11.1.21 Sure. Wonderful to hear this. Great start to a
fabulous New Year

1pm 19.1.21
Dishu whoops and yells as India lift trophy.

9am 19.1.21 Blissful Havan

6am 18.1.21
Woke from a delicious dream, fineness was sitting and all excited,
waiting for me to touch and get infused.

Infact even in the dream what was amazing is that she took the
front seat next to me replacing another girl.

1004pm 18.1.21
She said with great excitement I am yours, and enjoyed a long
hearty laugh savoring the sweetness of being my girlfriend.

12noon 17.1.21
Vastu consultation for plot no 145 overlooking Buddha Park.

16.1.21
happy b'day princess
438am 17.1.21 Thank you soooo much bhaiya for remembering and
your kind and loving wishes, always :) 🖤 :)

17.1.21
at times in the day, a very pleasant healing smell that reminded me
of long-ago fitness, and a feeling that I would again be fully fit.

11:16am to 1pm 21.1.21
Dishu grand Convocation
https://youtu.be/nZk3iZXHv8A

802am 1.1.21
Wishing you a beautiful and happy New Year. May this be a year of
Truth, Delight and Exemplary Works
809am Blessings n love. Arunachal
838am Same to you Ji. May God give you health & ultimate vision to
guide us. Happy New year HThapar
1121am *What Goes Around.. Comes Around* :)

May Lord in the New Year 2021 give you Joy Peace Vigor Resource Sanyam Purity Success Wealth Sadhana Sanskar and Health, Self, ♥ Life's fourfold aims Dharma Artha Kama Moksha, may with Lord's grace within this life you attain. Multifold Blessings. Infatuated.

137pm Wish you a very happy healthy and spiritually best and better than any other year. You achieve your goals. Jayanti n bhai

507pm May the new year and the coming decade brings happiness , good health, new perspective of life and amazing events in your and your loved one's lives. Happy new year 2020. Regards kj

910am 2.1.21 Dear Ashwani ji thanks and wish you too a very happy New Year 2021. Always wish and pray for your good health and happiness Regards and Best Wishes P K B

Grace Pours

Om namo bhagavate
         Dhanvantaraye
Amritakalasha hastāya
         Sarva bhaya vināshanāya
Trailokyanāthāya
         Shri Maha Vishnave Swāha

726am 11 Aug 20
Divine Devi Tripura Sundari a very happy, blissful, and satisfying
Janmashtami
8am Yha Janmashtami kal hai Prabhu. Happy Janmashtami to you

10am 21 Aug 20
Chatted with passionate love for an hour. Good tuning and
productive work together.

24 Aug 20
Lord in dream. Long dream. Good dream.

27 Aug 20
Evening Sunset told me - things are going fine for you in every way.
You shall experience freedom from guilt.fear.lack Jai Gurudev

2 Sep 2020
Our heartiest congratulations and blessings on our grandson
joining his job from today with the option to start working from
home as of now. It's nice that the company has provided a fully
programmed laptop to suit their requirement.

843am 5.Sep.2020

Teacher's Day beckons. Grateful Pranaams. Jai Gurudev ashwini

853am Vrunda. Jgd Kaise hae aap?

1012am Happy Teacher's Day to you too ♥ Tr

1018am Thanku so much. Same beckons for you too. Really, it's a great feeling. Delicate.

1046am Atukki Happy Teachers Day swami ji ....pranam

0830pm 3.9.20

Radha your voice is too sweet. I felt blessed on hearing your prayer chanting

348pm 8.9.20

Vo book mil gai hai

454pm Yes, it is nice

427am 8.9.20

Guardian Angel Yaksha directly above home. Clicked with moon. It is yellow, appears white in photo. Another photo has Venus directly in East.

Guardian Yaksha rises in East and travels in 1 hour to be above house. Noticed it since past week, appears like a moving aeroplane.

705am 11.9.20

Lord takes my name. Thank You Bhagvan Shiva.

Dec 1 2001 Bangalore Dalai Lama Guruji met. Said by PGupt.

103am 12.9.20

Thank you so much ashwiniji....

905pm 14.9.20
Devi ab to aap bahut khush hogi. Adhik Maas shuru ho raha hai
909pm Ji. Aaj bhi achha din tha. Sare Planets apne sthan pe hai.
Abhi kal aaj aur kal teen din sadhana ke liye bhot hi achhe hai.
7am 15.9.20 Devi many thanks for this valuable information.
Showers of Love on you. May your Sadhana be Successful. Feel the
Freedom and the Strength to do Great Tapasya and Noble deeds

17.9.20 Morning
The Chiku tree topped the fence, Amla tree is full of white flowers.

134pm 17.9.20
Today is Mahalaya Amavasya and we are having honey and cream
goodies
421pm Yes

825am 30.9.20
With your blessings he got his first pay. C

842pm 1.10.20
Namaste ji. How are you blissed out ? Hopefully your creative
energies are continuing and flowing out :) V
902pm Thanks very much. Gratefulness and Happyness
1021am 2.10.20 Sorry, if I had taken any longer time than you
anticipated in our divine conversation. I may have been a bit
carried away - when taking about Puṣpā! She is a giant, apārā viduṣī.
Nice to hear and reconnecting with you. Śubham bhavatu. V

413pm 2.10.20
Sir, that's a perfect birthday gift for Ashwini's mother. What a
typical yellow hue n flavour these galgals have. Above all she is
feeling a lot more energetic. It's unbelievable.

210pm 6.10.20
Consort called and poured love, showered blessings, a fantastic
AMC with Yogi.

730pm 7.10.20
Are you feeling better now? Dishu
737pm Yes certainly
748pm Glad. My exams start from Monday. I have been preparing
for them diligently. I also have started reading and giving short
explanations of Yoga Sutras in evening yoga sessions.
819pm That is the first step. Also spend few minutes playing cards
with Nanima
602pm 8.10.20 Yes mammu

1142am 8.10.20
Baby called and chatted freely lovingly, Mumbai had left.

1226pm 15.10.20
Golden in bliss, strong, clear hearted. Chatted in delight.

1231pm 15.10.20
Received yoga science and practice just now. Thanku. C

418pm 15.10.20
FD smoothly opened. Exciting.

3pm 15.10.20
Lord received YOGA Science and Practice. Thrilled.
7pm Guruji spoke cheerfully about Navratri.
730pm Amazing meditation, I am accepted by Lord Shiva the
Brahman in the Heart Lotus.

801pm 16.10.20 call
Consort in high heaven. Bubbling with Joy.

1114am 17.10.20 call
Flame is high profile now. Met Guruji 4 times in last 4 months.

Vertical Take Off.

952am 18.10.20
Pranaams Mataji. Navaratri refreshes the soul and renews the body.
https://youtu.be/MWK9-Ztl5j8 You are a Devi yourself
1019am Ashwini all best wishes and blessings for Navratri

730pm 22.10.20 Shasti

- Guruji showered Rich Blessings

- as Skand-mata, Mother is so relaxed and carefree

- as You her son shall take care of everything, annihilate all troubles.

730pm 23.10.20 Saptami
Khushmanda high Prana

The most Beautiful.

Gauri the purest, fairest in all matters

730pm 24.10.20 Ashtami
Lord says "Mother says you are liberated, even then if you feel troubled and weak, know that I Guruji am with You, and I am very strong, so no fear".

730pm 25.10.20 Navami
As Siddhi-datri, Mother gives material and spiritual wealth both.
Full blessings by Lord.

730pm 26.10.20 Dussehra
Go and be victorious. Gati means movement, attainment, liberation.

710pm 27.10.20
Thank you dear for your bday greetings...you have enriched my life
in so many ways ...thanks for the book on bhajagovindam and
yogasanas...very good books. Getup is also very good...shabaash
bete...lots of love and best wishes
809pm Mummy ji you make my heart glow. Love You

830pm 27.10.20
Strong hitchki palpable for 15 minutes, Intimacy made sweet love.

727pm 31.10.20
Trying to talk to you since last one week but somehow you are not
available for me. Your phone is constantly switched off and
sometimes it rings but you do not receive my call. Please call me...
Courier reached in Navratri's last day... Yesterday was Sharad
Purnima, my Diksha day... U didn't bless me.....
239pm 8.11.20 Dearie. Ji am very sorry for missing your calls. Please
forgive me. Lots of Love and Guru Grace for your Diksha tithi.

1245pm 7.11.20
J n J visit. Amazing Grace just as Lord's visit. Everyone thrilled and
contented.

6pm 8.11.20
Guru Puja Havan at W's. Nothing's changed, yet significant smiles.

846pm 8.11.20
Hoi Ashtami Puja. Your contribution...
Yoga Science and Practice, is such a significant piece of wisdom,
intellect and compassion for humanity....
I whole heartedly congratulate you for the same.
With Prayers. Limited nBound

914am 9.11.20
It is a significant Diwali for us all by Lakshmi Devi's august visit.

7pm an exquisitely beautiful brass idol of Mahalakshmi graced our home.

642am 13.11.20 Dhanteras
Tripura Sundari ki Jai. Shubh Deepawali.
651am Happy happy and limitless joyful Deepawali to you.

5pm 14.11.20
Lord blessed with a fabulous Diwali Puja.
8pm In Meditation he said, no worries, all abundance, everything has been taken care of.

1145am 15.11.20
Baby called happily. Looking very strong and confident after a great homa on Dhanteras 13th Nov.

10am to 7pm 18.11.20
Baby's Lakshmi Stotra book done. A very happy girl.

7pm 22.11.20 elyments video call
Lord appreciated my innovative work, great job and a lifetime of blissful peace. Thank You Guruji.

713pm 23.11.20
Dishu called to say font work is done. Amazing Success. 2 months of dogged hard work has paid off. Thank You Guruji.

745pm 26.11.20
One Student already purchased it. Will wait for its release on 28th. Tr

3.12.20

A day when I finally have a new life in a new plane. Things are gonna be different from today. There shall be hope, freedom, lightness and peace.

Night Sleep 5.12.20

Radha and Lord in a long dream. Lord is part of our family, and seems entirely human and homely.

8:30am 6.12.20

At morning milk time, J remarks I am healed, and sure enough I feel fit. Seems that Lord really wants me well.

Early morning 7.12.20

Before waking up had a great time with Milk Maiden. Then after waking up in the shower got news she had come to stay here. Of course I visited her and we replayed our time with intimacy of fineness.

Night bedtime 7.12.20

After many many years the fluid was rich, luxuriant and plentiful, shining and glistening.

As if in deep awe, the body glowed, infused with new life.

Got an incredible release and freedom.

10:30am 8.12.20

Doc saw my hands and patted, it was just a silly something that would be gone in five days.

1.39pm 9.12.20

Lo and behold, as I get out of the car, a big package of new pillows!!!

Ji many many thanks for the pillow.
649pm Welcome Bhaiya.

238pm 12 Dec 2020
Today, it looks you were so busy... Is everything ok?
Thank you so much for coffee order. Since 3 months, I was thinking
to order online but was unable to do....... Thanks 🖤

13 Dec 2020
- Started watching Guruji's talks after getting the iPod AV
  cable, been a long time...

- Received an amazing info from J regarding competitor.

- First time my book bought and appreciated by a Bangalore
  ashramite.

- Golden buys univ domain.

14 Dec 2020
Since I woke up, I am feeling good, free, no stress. It's a light feeling
since a long long time. Thank You Bhaiya.

1039am 15.12.2020
Happy Vedanta conversation with J. Priceless.

1216pm 18.12.20
First time beloved said I'm in love with you,
in a long happy amorous chat.

Early morning 19.12.20
Long dream of grace, attention, respect, responsibility, good will.

Evening 19.12.20
Lord graced my mind, absorbed me within, led me by the hand,
reaffirmed that I am his.

Got a good pair of chappals and socks, movement and rest both.

Dream 24.12.20
In a rare dream today morning was solving some complex physics equation...

1001am 25.12.20
Pranaams Mataji. It is our great good fortune that Lord gave us the nectar of Bhagavad Gita. Jai Gurudev
504pm Yes Ashwini all love and best wishes on Gita Jayanti.

533pm 27.12.2020
I got the Mudra rahasya book. It's really very nice and useful too
650pm Radha how was Gita Parayan?
705pm Nice 🖤 we did in morning 8:30 to 11:00am

340pm 28.12.20
Hopefully you can publish Rudra Tattva eBook? Wishing you a fantastically successful Happy New Year
449pm DhanyavaadaH for the positive kaamanaa. Much gratitude. Sai

Cool Down Slow Down

- wake up 330am
- Clean rooms and shelves with bhasma. apply vinegar too.
- Padmasadhana Twice daily

Dhyanamulam Gururmurtih Pujamulam Gururpadam.
Mantramulam Gururvakyam Mokshamulam Guruh Kripa.

Detox Diet

7am Green Coconut Water/Triphala Water

9am White Pumpkin juice

11am Breakfast with Seasonal Fruits

2pm Lunch with Roti Subzi

     prepare roti with 50% atta and 50% millet

4pm Salad Snack

6pm Gourd juice

8pm Dinner with Soup and Moong Dal

     can interchange Lunch with Dinner.

10/7/2018
Bhagavad Gita verses 4.11, 4.12
Sanskrit dhatu vid lat iii/1, srip dhatu sarp lot ii/1
bahuvrihi mixed up with Tatpurusha samasa.

On 5th March 1981 Gurudev gave us the 1st Sudarshan kriya, exactly
37 years ago. 5/3/2019 Morning Rudra Homa.

Feeling Good

125pm 7.6.20
Strong scent of Chandan for many minutes while sitting on J's
office sofa

1028pm 9.6.20
Dearie feels passionate affectionate lovely.

11am 10.6.20
Raindrops cool breeze flame lit throughout. Sitting in freshly
ploughed field. Temple and Residential prayer for residency.

310pm 13.6.20
Radha Avtar book mil gyi hai. Thank you prabhu

1228pm 16.6.20
Radha did you read the books? Do you like it Devi?
256pm Radha Avtar is a wonderful book. Really nice and readable.

5-14 June 20
6.6.20 GuruPuja Havan deep's. Then in CosmoC.

7.6.20 9am to noon
An extraordinary day. Prayers at

- CosmoC
- new office
- new market plaza restaurants (couple of black goats
  appeared from nowhere heralding tremendous footfall)
- new residency and new temple - an incredible play of nature
  - very windy yet lamp was lit - then cool drizzle - finally clear
  blue sky
- new school area

- children's grassy lawn opposite new clubhouse - almost noon yet sun was mild though bright, drizzle too
- finally at Ferozepur Road commercial complex giveaway.

9.6.20
daman took me home after 7pm to watch Narad Bhakti Sutra.

10.6.20
online group sadhana short kriya with sanyam too. Then to green park for Hindi Bhakti Sutra. Here I completed the Yoga book color plates.

20.6.20
A golden day for me. This thought stayed with me.

3pm 27.6.20 Yoga Book
Bharya adores and calls happily. Yoga poses are something. Remarkable.

27.6.20
Guru Gita the complete exposition. 5-7pm G3 session.
Hairline sensation in left side of brain. Enough vibrations in body, clenching of palms.

my new wooden cot plan finalized. Wow.

415am 30.6.20
Gurudev we wish you very happy birthday & many many happy returns of the day. We are fortunate to have great & enlightened soul like you in our life.
726am I am feeling happy and light. Thank You ji. The nature also rejoices when the sangat is together

817am 30.6.20
A very very happy bday dear bhai. Stay healthy n blessed always. C
817am Yes, many thanks. Weather is also nice and rainy

1102am Happy birthday dear bhaiya... stay blessed always. Delicate

931am 1.7.20
Wow. That's a long-time overdue meeting. See you soon. Aaj to ek wonderful girl ka birthday hai ..
414pm Thanku aap ki behn hoon na isliye

541pm
Shiva called and it was most divine talking for 17min 17sec

741pm
Ma'am served delicious hot food 24min

1019pm
Hello bhaiyaaaa....wish you a very very happy birthday ji :) hope you had a great one...lots of love and best wishes from me and d :)
1043 Am feeling so nice and fortunate that the Princess blessed me

1039pm
Long chat with a happy Limited nBound on home remedies.
1042pm Wow. Fabulous. Thanks Lakshmi ji. Grateful Pranaams. Will be in touch regarding our Ayurveda book

1042pm
Wish you a very happy birthday dear Mont ♥ pleasure bharya
1043pm Yeh hui na baat. Wah!

1057pm
Many Many Happy Birthday Mont GBU.
Thank You. I am thrilled to get your sms

849am 1.7.20
Consort called thrillingly. Wants to do VTP and become teacher.

1010am 2.7.20
Golden called having determined her new professional life.

1145am 2.7.20
Dwarka Temple called saying they thoroughly liked Shiv Puran and got it right on time.

Noon 6.7.20
First day of Shravan. First Monday Rudra Puja K D. Felt a wave of peace, and a tranquil fitness.

1030pm 6.7.20
Sir I had new idea about thirty-three crore devi devta. Please check is it right way of thinking? Let's say human life is of 100 years & if we divide 33 crore by hundred it becomes 33 lakhs & divide that by 365 days & then by 24 hours. It means 6 thoughts per hour i.e. one thought in ten minutes serves as a devta, to be followed. I may be wrong but shared with you as it strikes.
730am 7.7.20 Your thinking is valid and excellent. 33 is a significant number in Vedas. Even in Guru Granth Sahib the Japji Sahib is present 33 times. There are basically 33 consonants in Hindi alphabet from "ka" to "ha". The trinity and it's powers = 3+3 is written as 33 just as we say 1+1 = 11 in our common phrase.

822pm 9.7.20
JGD Ashwini bhai, your books got delivered an hour ago. Thanks a lot. Shiva Benign Earth.
915pm My grateful Pranaams. Hoping you enjoy atleast a bit.

9am 12.7.20 Sunday
MnM another Rudra Puja superbly organized with reaffirmation of deep peace and fitness.

8:30am 16.7.20
New start to a saloon that grows and a Rudra Abhishek that spreads great good cheer, that makes Ludhiana the undisputed best city with highest innovations, inventions, creative work force and respect for human values, Indian traditions and yogis.

331pm 16.7.20
Muscle name - Flexor hallucinate longus. Swami ji gopica
938pm Grateful Thanks. All the very best

1059pm 16.7.20
Jai Gurudev Dwarka Gujarat. Aapki bheji 3 books mil gayi. Hum log
bahut lucky hai jo aapke jaise saral, saumya, aur pratbhishali
peronality ke aashirwaad ke saath hai. Thanks bhaiya for all.
1007am 17.7.20 Happy to get your sms. Hope you enjoy reading the
books. Jai Gurudev

139pm 17.7.20
Drum practice is very good and will appeal to all in the long run
206pm Thank you mammu.

10am 19.7.20
J's J visited Green Park for the first time and chatted carefree,
feeling totally at home.

11am 19.7.20
An exceedingly fine Puja very well organized and performed by DMC
n Shankara, who were pleased with it and chatted happily
afterwards.

8am 20.7.20 Sompati Masya Rudra Puja.

5pm dreamt that I was speaking to Guruji. He said that the main
Bluetooth transmitter cable had an insulation tear in the dense
undergrowth. I replied to Guruji that I could patch the connection
and to show me where the cut was. Then we both started going
down the stairs. I was striding down in jumps and I noticed Guruji
doing the same, he was just behind. A thought came that I should
reduce my pace and make it comfortable for him. Also that I
shouldn't be in front.

Then the dream ended and I sat up. With a clear recollection of the
entire dream, including scenery, speech, thoughts and emotions.

And clear presence of Guruji.

935am 27 July 20
Devi aaj aapki yaad aa rahi hai. Today it is Shravan Somvar so you must be busy in Rudra Puja. Aap to Bhagwan ki param Bhakt ho. Lots of Happiness, Wisdom, Strength and Cheerfulness for you
232pm Ji aaj Laghu Rudra kiya. Subah 3 hours pooja chali. Mumbai bhi hai to vo bhi thi pooja me...

Beech me ek din phone kiya tha lekin Aap nhi mile...
Hope you are fine. All is well? 24th tarikh ko phone kiya tha.

31 July 20
Woke up with a clear recollection of a long dream in which Guruji was there all throughout. Nothing much happened, it was just a close physical presence. Reassuring.

338pm 2.8.20
Sri Sri Sir,
Myself a-deep, California messaging you, got your reference from Art of living group, was hoping to talk to you regarding learning. Sanskrit & Bhagavad Geeta, when is a good time to call you? Looking forward to hearing from you! Sri Sri

1107pm 4.8.20
Ji. I got the ghee. Please do not do much expense for me... You take care of yourself....
1157pm It is pure and fresh. Hope you like it. Sweet Dreams.

642am 5.8.20
Good morning. But it is so costly also...
1006am Devi it is made in Ashram with love. The calf is first given the milk and then we take. The cows roam freely and eat the correct plants and herbs.
1008am Aapko printer ink bhi mili?
1107am Ji. Vo to maine msg kiya tha. Prabhu

9am 5 Aug 20 to 950am
My university begins with very first California online class.
8 Aug 20
Felt unwell all day. At night heard that Bapi of Som had left for heavenly abode early morning.

4pm 9 Aug 20
Front treeline Bamboo fencing done. The entire home has a light fresh pleasant and divine look!

10 Aug 20
A supreme day of untold abundant grace. 728am 11 Aug 20.

27 Oct 2019 Diwali

7pm 27/10/2019
Guruji live from Vasad Ashram. Mummy happily came and sat on the sofa and enjoyed thoroughly.

Guruji said take whatever wish you want. It shall be granted. Jai Gurudev

847am 31/10/2019
A very sacred Unity Divas. Jai Gurudev
854am We are one. Arunachal

904am Aapko bhi aseem shubh kaambayen...
Pranaam. Jai Gurudev! Limited nBound

907am Dear up-karakam. Happy Unity Divas. Jai Gurudev ashwini
919am Same to you dear

7pm 28/10/2019
Mahalakshmi Ashtakam chanting in online presence of Guruji Mumbai.

Guruji said now close the eyes for mantra snan. All pain grief shall be banished. Sri Suktam homa 15min.

1110am 29/10/2019
Baby called and spoke for 20min. Relaxed at ease.

New year started yesterday, 28th Oct. Her parents and foreign stayed with her for 5 days prior to and until Diwali.

Visited Maa on 13th Oct Sharad Poornima diksha day. Will visit again 28th Dec to 1st Jan 2020 for Maa's platinum jubilee birthday.

Nourishment

1056am 31.12.19
RThapar called to say if I could come to Raikot for Puja on New Year's Day. Wow!

Mummy also accompanied, climbed a long flight of steep steps, and thoroughly enjoyed the drive to Raikot, Ludhiana, and back home the next day.

528pm 31.12.19
Consort called and chatted happily.

441pm 31.12.19
Om namah shivaya. Jai Gurudev
443pm Thank u Swami ji, we all love you a lot. W

201pm 2.1.20
Dearie called and said Jai Gurudev in a cheery crisp voice and wished Happy New Year.

729pm 2.1.20
Brilliance of Purity and Wisdom Happiness 2020
947pm Gratitudes, prayers and regards. Shubh 2020. Limit unBound

733pm 2.1.20
Brilliance of Purity and Wisdom Happiness 2020

639am 3.1.20
How are you ? All well ?
1152am Yes Rishiji. Am very happy and enjoying Guruji's Grace. Writing my Sanskrit Grammar books
1158am Very good

6.1.20 All Morning
Publishing Company registered at Sirhind Road Secretariat office.
7.1.20 manufacturing Updated to Services on website.
8.1.20 ProfnSons company Bliss
Mundaka Upanishad started

9.1.20
Simi fixing FF East Verandah. K D clears Hall of throwaway.
629pm Mangrul happy couple sang a song.

10.1.20 Poornima

1233pm 10.1.20
Okay mammu. I will shift upstairs today and also make timetable.
Enjoy the world book fair.
228pm I feel a timetable will ensure regular sadhana. I will start
with that today
302pm Goody. Go for it

1056pm 14.1.20
Sorry I missed your call...how are you..it is long since you came
home to us...please come..good night
251am 15.1.20 Ok mummyji. Shall come.

115pm 16.1.20
Birthday Princess showers us all with delights
138pm Oh Bhaiya, thank you soooo much for your sweetest
wishes...come soon to Mumbai...all December we were thinking
about you how you were with us in 2018 :) take care ji, Khudahafiz :)

Meditate 2019

813am 1 Jan 2019
Sir I wish you happy & prosperous new year.
May your enlightenment shine more & bless the world with treasures of spirituality.
I feel blessed to have GURU & Friend like you .
826am Thank you ji. Feeling blessed, grateful and enriched with your caring Friendship.
Greetings and love for A , A , S.
Pranaams to J , M. Sat Sri Akal.

447pm 6/1/2019
Thanks Nanu. i enjoyed immensely
517pm So did I. Thank you for coming. :))

857pm 6/1/2019
Jgd Three days of Dhyanostav with BhanuD in Thane. Had Tr 's meet with her and celebrated her birthday today.
905pm Dearest Teacher the grace showers on its beloved devotee in ways that the human mind gets liberated.

502pm 16/1/2019
Happyness Birthday Princess
520pm Thank you so much dearest Bhaiya :):)

451pm 18/1/2019
Please call when free. Consort
9pm Consort spoke with lots of freedom and excitement regarding
school in plainWaters.

217pm 22/1/2019
Really wonderful..... I never knew that I was always talking to a big
Big gyani..... Lovely collections.... Now I can get answers for all my
questions from you.

Sure I would love to read the books. Thank you. BabliK
827pm Thank you very much. Feeling blessed by your praises.

753pm 22/1/2019
Baby called and spoke cheerfully for 10min, fully occupied with
packing and vibrantly youthful.
833pm Thank you Radha. Your voice is so happy and filled with
goodness of divinity.

827am 23/1/2019
Devi with your permission I can visit for a couple of days.
1132am Kab?? On Shivaratri or on Vastu pooja 21st February??
1149am i was thinking if you need help i can come on 27th Jan
1157am For need I cannot call you from so far... And Mumbai and
three more people are coming for shifting... That is not an issue.....

917pm 22/1/2019
Yes. Got the book. Thanks dear.
944pm ok Mummyji. Love you.

744am 23/1/2019
I came back from Calicut yesterday night so this delay in
responding. book has come out well. bauji will be happy. how are
you doing?

1026am Doing well Mummyji. Happy and engrossed in my Sanskrit
work. Missing you too.

858am 25/1/2019
SSA Swami ji, Thanks for your love & care always

542pm 9/2/2019
Dear Respected Swamiji. a pious purifying and joyous Basant
Panchami. Jai Gurudev
730pm Very Glad to get the Message Ashwani ji Maharaj. At
Chhatisgarh now for 4 days. Wish you too a Blissful Basant
Panchami. May Goddess Saraswati enlighten our intellect.
Remembering the time we spent together at Academy.
750pm Param Pujya Swamiji. I feel thrilled to receive your loving
reply. Thank you so much.

532am 15/2/2019
Jai GuruDev Bhaiya
We shall be picking you anytime between 7:30 and 8 AM today.
Good morning!
701am Sure. A wonderful morning.
Spent an excellent day at Univ across Panini Mahavidyalaya, and
Oshodhara.

924am 19/2/2019
Oh, thanks for my gift. Your friendship (like Krishna to Arjuna) and
loving guidance are my gifts that I will treasure always. VLord

12pm 19/2/2019
Sir thanks for great gift in form of books. I am delighted to have this
great knowledge by revered & enlightened guru "shri A A ji ". I am
fortunate to have such great soul as my intimate friend. Thanks
once again.
1208pm Sat Sri Akal ji. Friendships are precious and enduring.

710pm 20/2/2019
No network. Was nice talking to you after a long time. Jgd ♥
711pm Jai Gurudev. Happyness and Cheerfulness in your voice
719pm Thank you. It's so true. All because of Guruji's grace. I'm so

lucky, fortunate & blessed.

1256pm 21/2/2019
Saffron Mudita calls me over to sit beside him on sofa as Snow
White is doing Vastu Shanti Puja.

756pm 21/2/2019
Consort is excited upon my visit.

823pm 21/2/2019
Victory on way to pick you. What a pleasant surprise.

232pm 27/2/2019
Wish you happy journey.... Sorry for less passionate affectionate
hospitality to you...
248pm Devi you are perfect in every way. You are the living Goddess.
Please live happily. Wish your Maha Shivratri is grand and filled with
abundant Blessings.

1130am 27/2/2019
Lord gives darshan and gestures as i come in shuttle from
Reception and he is coming from Ganga and going down North
Road towards Yagnashala entrance for Patanjali Yoga Sutras.

1030am 1/3/2019
First hollow and empty meditation in AMP is very deep.

11pm 3/3/2019
Lord passes then halts, sees me and comes back to pat with his
rose. Row sitting in Yagnashala.

12noon 4/3/2019 Maha Shivratri
5elements dissolve in Shiva principle meditation. It is superb.
2pm after lunch Git is standing there all smiles.
6pm after longKriya in Yagnashala there is Teachers Meet and Git
hands over Bhagavad Gita Applied Wisdom to Lord.

1130pm 4/3/2019
Just after a superb Tandava and before his OmNamahShivaya

Meditation 1145 to 1215am, Lord says we are all taken care of well. Our efforts shall yield fruit. Our fondest hopes shall come true.

3am 5/3/2019
Lord is all smiles sitting on chair as i pass by in darshan line in Yagnashala.
5am Rudra Homa followed by Rudra Puja at GuruPadukaVanam.

351pm 7/3/2019
How are you Ashwani ji Maharaj. Received your loving gift of Ishavasya Upanishad.
356pm Pranaams Swamiji. We are in Shivratri bliss and am working on my Sanskrit. Many thanks for your inspiring words. Jai Gurudev

907am 15/3/2019
Your bits bookings have been done. Please don't tell him.

257pm 16/3/2019
I got evaluation call for 4th and 5th May 2019 from marma desk.
302pm great news. go for it. and enjoy Vigyan Bhairav. it is very powerful

Guruji's Punjab visit. So stormy and elevating as well. 15th Chd. 16th Panchkula. 17th Ludhiana. 18th Bathinda.

18/3/2019 Bathinda Satsang 5-8pm
in one fell sweep Guruji removed all blocks. showered grace. 2Boys came over to our home from gurudwara. Happy and grateful.

12midnight 21/3/2019 BITS Pearl
for the first time saw and properly enjoyed the dance performances, and it felt good.

737pm 22/3/2019
Happy Holi from BITS campus
738pm Happy Holi ji:)
How are you? Are you in Hyderabad!?! Swami's daughter

645pm 23/3/2019 5pm Audi
Saw a play in Pearl. in it the girl reminded me of you...her talking, smiling, movements...seemed it was the Princess.
1018am 24/3/2019 Awww...Thank you for your sweet kind message bhaiya :):) Hope you are doing well...Take care ji 🖤

31st March Lord gave me Satsang.

1st April he gave a most refreshing day with intro-talk and Vastu.

2nd April was GuruPuja with 114 attendees! Thankyou Bhaiya. i felt normal and cared for.

609pm 3/4/2019
graceful beautiful pleasant birthday eve Dearest Monica
616pm Thanks so much

1240pm 4/4/2019
got the document made to her highness's exacting standards.
553pm Thank you so much
557pm Tripura Sundari you are perfect

Lord showered too much love. i felt alive, wanted, employed, and nourished.

7:30pm 13/4/2019 Rewari
Strong Chandan smell evening sanyam. and what a fabulous get-together. We laughed and laughed and laughed.

1124am 14/4/2019 Baisakhi Bliss Swamiji
103pm Everything here is Mortal, Only our Lord is Immortal. For a Sadhak everyday is Ramanavami & Everyday is Guru Purnima. Let's Live in this Spirit. Jai Gurudev
106pm Yes sure Param Pujya Swamiji. Fully agree with the dedication needed by a sadhaka. Perhaps you received Narada Bhakti Sutra book?
110pm Yes Yes I think I have already Conveyed, may be that

Message has not reached. Any how it's very nice that you have clarified the meaning with splitting the words.

5pm 16/4/2019
Meditation Chair arrived. Bharya overpowered with excitement.

543pm 16/4/2019
Sat Sri Akal. Welcome Home. We shall meet another time as i am away for Pujas. Hope you have a fruitful and enjoyable visit. Jai Gurudev.

28/4/2019 Home
Such a wonderful welcome. Thank you very much Bhaiya. The day became divine with Sunny Enclave visit with guru lala. Mummy smiled a lot and played dussar. Dishu's ipad "renovated" to laptop.

7/5/2019 Akshay Tritiya Long Kriya
Lord called in the form of Consort. Her mother and Victory. plainWaters.

13/5/2019 Tera May.
Lord came home for some fine cooking.
Nanu's brand new Chromebook received.
One to one darshan after morning Rudra Puja in Yagyashala.

1042am 21/5/2019
Dear Anna. many smiles and successes on a happy birthday.
1046am Dear Ashwini Bhaiya. Jai Gurudev. Thank you very much. I am feeling grateful to have you in my life. Regards. Ayurveda

432pm 24/5/2019
Ok sir, thanks for visiting us. We feel blessed to have your company.
433pm I also feel great to meet you.

505pm 29/5/2019
Radha please sms iPhone model no. Also there is one number at back of phone.

539pm Abhi karen kya? Mujhe nhi aata dekhna. A1778. iphone 7 gsm. 256gb.

1020am 29/5/2019
Om namo narayanaaya, ganga Dussehra will be celebrated in Sri Kailas Ashram and branches on June 12th. Pujya Maharaj Shree will be discoursing on Gita from 11th to 18th June 2019 at Sri Kailas Ashram, Uttarkashi. We invite you and family for the same. For details you may contact Swamiji.

1138am 3/6/2019
our Teak wood is Gir Lion color. the best.
1148am Architect uncle also says the contrast looks good. The natural color is soothing.

1001am 16/6/2019
Can I get your help? Please...
18 calls and DewDrop is in 7th heaven.
229pm yes sure Radha.

noon 17/6/2019
J's J successfully completes 7-day GM diet. Waistline 1.5inch trim 5kg weight loss and cheery mood.

500pm 17/6/2019
Mummy is very happy you visited.
519pm The happiness is both sided.

18/6/2019 past midnight 108am
The moon came out of the clouds to nourish me and shower seeds on fineness.

21/6/2019 IDY night
Lord came in long dream. And ate happily. Even Darling was present.

22/6/2019
Call from Nabha. All my karmas wiped clean.

23/6/2019
Call from Admin of Shantikunj Shimla.

24/6/2019
May you shine like a million suns and may your effulgence spread far and wide. HAPPY BIRTHDAY. Koti Koti Pranaams to Guru Maa.

27/6/2019 1034am
Baby calls up all ready to date.
5pm after JioFi activation.
Honey played 2 youtube music videos for me. Second was chal akela chal akela by Mukesh. She's enthralled.
600pm Thank you.
754pm Her brand-new MI is functional as she connects and signs off.

1055am 30/6/2019
Lord called from Ashram while in Delhi!

956am 1/7/2019
Sir wish you very happy birthday & many many happy returns of the day. We are fortunate to have company of great divine soul like you. Your presence in our life is greatest asset for us.
1017am Friends are the good fortune in everyone's life. Thank you very much.

7pm 2/7/2019 Bday Blessing
Ayush Homa at Ludhiana TOK with Rishiji. Bathinda drive and back.

818pm 5/7/2019
9th std calls to express thrill at her story being selected in publisher's anthology.

528am 13/7/2019
Mummyji visiting Shimla. Could you please sms bhaiya's contact.
550am That is good. Hope You Are Doing Fine. go to Sanjouli Bazar.
Enjoy.

617am 13/7/2019
Devi aap khush ho na. Please do not hesitate to ask for anything.
756am Main Thik hun. Thanks

1143am 16/7/2019
JGD! Happy Guru Poornima 🖤 Was trying to call you. Call when you
are free. Consort.
958am 17/7/2019 Thank you so much. A most blessed Guru
Poornima and Shravan Season.

18th night
Lord comes in a long dream. He's in charge. It is all super smooth.

1133am 20/7/2019
Thank You Sri, I'm cleansed through and through...
753pm
i'm sure Satsang vibrations heal many layers of creation
630am 21/7/2019 Yes Sri 🖤 deep healing took place.

844am 21/7/2019
Happy days are here again SSS.
1140am Thanks Ashwini. With friends like you, happy days last year
long.

512am 30/7/2019
Devi aapko Shravan Rudra Puja ka bharpur labh aur aashirvad
954am Ji. Thanks 🖤 Aap kaise hai??
956am Spoke to Baby Beauty for 9 min. Such a happy kid she is.

526pm 8/8/2019
Yes thank you so much I was too busy travelling for Pujas, the
books are really very well made, a treasure JGD. Calcutta.
528pm Thankyou Swamiji. You are very welcome. Jai Gurudev

130pm 18/8/2019
A fine AnandUtsav completed.
639pm the birds are singing and the breeze is happily waving. such a fine evening. Ashwini
639pm Golden. ♥ wakefulness
648pm So true...Divinity everywhere. Blessings!!! Limited unBound.
648pm So true. Bharya humility
7pm Jgd Swamiji, I'm also outside listening to birds enjoying nature walk at home. K-bir
702pm Yes dear, we had an amazing experience at Anand Utsav Ambarnath. Tr
715pm Navy Admiral Mamaji
716pm It's a wonderful life!!! Sai
849pm Yes weather is really nice these days.... Gurgaon
849pm It surely is. It's also Laxmi's birthday. W's J.

0218am 19/8/2019 This message filled me with such unadulterated joy @ Nanu.
928am Hello Ashwini ji. Enjoying the nature and its creations. God bless. Jullundur.
404pm Ashwini thanks for remembering Hope you must be alright and enjoying the life. Best wishes. P K B
804am 20/8/2019 I see! You have reached the ashram. Cooed my dainty slim peacock Bharya.

Seems all is a Dream

4am 19/8/2019

Guruji came in my dream. He was visiting some Ashram. As he entered reception the fan made something (flame??) difficult. He looked at me and gestured and i turned off the fan switch. Then he tugged at Vishnu and Vishnu followed him to his room. Everyone applauded.

The wonderful dream continued with a child happily playing. Towards the end we were in a hall with men sitting on chairs in a row. And in the opposite row people standing. Guruji arrived and briefly spoke to 3 men one of whom pointed at me and said my name. Then Guruji went to the sitting men and greeted them one by one. He also touched the feet of one man towards the end. Then he came to our row. I was in the group at the start. He immediately came to me and said - How are you Ashwini? - and shook my hand and then i touched His feet. He moved to greet other people. The young girl chatted with him happily.

730am Greeted by a fine morning with the sun out and a drizzle. And such a beautiful rainbow with colors violet-indigo-blue clearly distinguished.

153pm 22/8/2019
joined AMC course so will come on Sunday 25ᵗʰ
219pm Wonderful mammu. Have a great time.

343pm 25/8/2019
Thanks for a great course and a wonderful time
1133pm We too enjoyed the course and your company. Will call you tomorrow. Consort

545pm 25/8/2019
a most grace filled AMC at Rishikesh Ashram. Hope to see you another time. All the Best
550pm JGD Bhaiya. Sure we will meet next time ♥ Winnipeg

546pm 25/8/2019
Mummyji am crossing Roorkee. Remembered you. After a profound Meditation course in our Rishikesh Ashram.
1049pm Great...when r u coming home?
523pm 26/8/2019 sure will visit Mummyji. whenever you are free and available.
747pm Most welcome always.. decide some date and ask me one week before. Lots of love.
1118am 28/8/2019 wow Mummyji. Love You

3pm 28/8/2019
Please call when free. Waiting to give you good news. Vi got job in london. Consort

431pm 31/8/2019
I will be at Sunny Enclave new home.
448pm Wow! Half an hour Sri

8pm 3/9/2019
Wah! Sri! With you came another wave of healing!

604am 8/9/2019

Sri, that LG TV we saw came home yesterday evening. How rightly you said if dark isn't pure eyes don't get rest. Watching the TV truth percolated in...

17/9/2019 Yes Jee. Guess TV is another example of your instinct in taking good care of family and generosity

126pm 5/9/2019

Happy Teacher's Day beloved teacher

810pm Thanks dear Wishing you the same. I have been overwhelmed by all the lovely messages today from all over. Tr

1126pm 5/9/2019

Happy Teachers Day from contented and lucky students from all across the globe.

1116am 6/9/2019 Thank you dear...delighted to have students like You!

1122am 6/9/2019

Mom is the first teacher to her children. Happy Teachers Day darling mother.

1134am Thanks so much ?? Monica

1014am 7/9/2019

Radha ki jai. Radhashtami ki badhai

1052am Thanks 🖤 Koi samachar nhi???? Sab thik hai na?

1053am Yes ji was remembering you too much.

151pm Kabhi kisi din chand pe jayenge

152pm Ji jrur jana. Vha se photos bhejna

153pm Abhi jo video bheja hai wo to dekh lo pehle

156pm Dekha. Kuchh samajh nhi aaya. Kal vali video nhi hai kya?

159pm Yeh 22 july ki hai. Chandrayaan2

208pm Aur yeh aaj subah ki hai 2am Saturday 7 Sept.
922pm OK I watched all these. I liked to watch.
922pm Thanks very much Devi. You made me happy

13/9/2019 Amazing Grace.
Sandhi Book submitted and got published in
america.bangalore.europe same day. Even one book got sold!

17/9/2019 Pouring of Grace.

- Mummy smiled. Talked happily. Ate well.

- Bharya with Adoration filled eyes called excitedly. Her loveFilled is engaged to a foreigner.

- In Kriya 10 participants and felt very light.

19/9/2019
Mummy wished to give donation. We gave Rs500 in the concluding bhagvat saptah bhandara at Hanuman Mandir parshuram chowk. Then ssrvm sent an email on this very day for donating to children. We donated Rs2000 for 1 child's transport for 1 full year.

21/9/2019
Mummy got hair oil applied and combed hair. In the evening she participated in Satsang and Meditation live with Guruji & AshaB.

22/9/2019 Evening
An elephant visited. Stopped at our home for 5min.

946pm 22/9/2019
Live PM in America now.

1056am 23/9/2019 Equinox
Thanks prabhu ♥ I watched it at night already
1114am Blessed are thee tripura sundari
1221pm Today is very Divine and Powerful day. It is Equinox. Today both day and night are equal of 12 hours duration each.
200pm ♥ you.

730am 23/9/2019
Mummy chopped ramtori vegetable and read the newspaper. Wow.

7am 24/9/2019
Til Homa with Rishiji at Rajpura. Bathinda people attended the same evening at 7pm.

7pm 24/9/2019
Til Homa made my body feel energized and fit. Infused peace and strength in the mind. Jai Gurudev. Grateful pranaams. Ashwini

706pm 25/9/2019
Good. Good. Good. Great and Graceful. Lots and Lots of Love and Blessings. Rishiji

640pm 26/9/2019
Jaipur called excited. 9th std's story published and she received copy of book. Will be available online!

730am 28/9/2019 Amavasya
Hooray! Mummy did short sudarshan kriya of her own free will.

9/10/2019
Brahman visited. Lord Krishna touched.
The last time it was on 26/11/2018.

Felt so much at ease. Without any reason. Entire day in peace.

Mummy

730am 11/10/2019
Smilingly Mummy said, "i am going out to have a stroll".

- For the whole of the next two years, she walked rounds around the home driveway.

- Also did many yogasanas and sang songs and read the daily newspaper and watched TV.

- Participated in Rudra Puja, Havan, and Festivals with gusto.

- Daily read the Bhagavad Gita and occasionally the Bhagavatam.

- Laughed and played dussar with children.

- Visited Chandigarh, Bathinda, Ludhiana, Samana and folks in Patiala.

- Enjoyed having her cot outside in the open sunshine during winters.

- Enjoyed watching the trees and plants, and the stars every night.

- Greeted the sun at dawn.

- Made cotton wicks for the lamps.

- Did occasional sewing and stitching work and veggie chopping and pruning.

Darling Radha

822am 23/9/2017
Most respected lovely Devi - Holy Geeta book parcel will come
Today. (Please inform security person if you go out).
1152am Sorry ji I didn't see your msg because there is some
problem with that SMS..... But thank God that 5minutes before I
started for the hospital, came... I got it... Thanks ji.. ..otherwise it
would have gone back...
1203pm O Radha, your tapasya is too strong. You shall always get it.
213pm Waw I am so happy.... Thank you so much dear...
432pm It will help me a lot.
742pm Ji Radha. Your feet are lotus and your words are amrit.

753pm 25/9/2017
Devi chand is too beautiful like you. Did you see?
813pm It's not seen from here
840pm Bhagavad Gita Sadhak Sanjivani Swami Ram Sukh Das.
https://gitapressbookshop.in/
928pm Ji.... amreliswamiji ne sadhak sanjivani ke liye bhi kaha tha
aaj....lekin maine aapse kha nhi.. Socha ki yahan kahin se dhundh
loongi........ YOU are great..
swamiji bol ke gaye the ki pehale adhyay me kam aayegi 🤍
931pm ji when you were speaking at that time i noticed your voice
was changed. It was very light very bright just like Shankaracharya.
931pm Yahan ki Geeta press se le aaungi
1009pm ji Tripura Sundari i am feeling happy. i am feeling strong.
Thankyou ji. Charan Sparsh
858pm 26/9/2018
Radha chand aa gaya hai. Beautiful Face. your eyes are sparkling
and cheeks are pink. so lovely
154pm 27/9/2018 OK thanks..
326pm 30/9/2018 What???

all day 6/10/2018
i feel light bright cheerful silent - brahman consciousness

900am 7/10/2018
Sunday walk towards DAshram along Ganges. At one point midway the Ganges waters come to me full of love.

afternoon night 8/10/2018
the pangs of bitterness and the thongs of fear and revulsion have a field day - good that they could be well received. In between at dinnertime 7pm a strong bout of hitchki someone was remembering.

1314pm 9/10/2018 Amavasya
i tie the knot with Beloved, under the twin banyan trees below Vishwanath mandir overlooking the Ganges.

209pm 9/10/2018
Jai Gurudev. Be Blissful in Thy Divine Grace. Dev bhakt ananda 209pm Om Namah Shivaya. Pranaams at thy lotus feet.

231pm 9/10/2018
Jaigurudev Ashwini bhai, thank you, I have received the book just now, very nice, very easy to learn shloka, Good good - Ved Niketan 239pm Jai Gurudev Swamiji. Aapki mahima apram paar. Thanks ji for blessings.

1042am 10/10/2018
- Sow the seed of Self-discipline

- Water it with Love.

- Fence it with the Lord's Name.

- The tree will yield you the fruit of Immortality. Swami Sivananda

1042am Yes Swamiji. Sure. Your words are most beneficial like amrita.

1148am 10/10/2018 Navratri Starts
Will think about..... I want some beautiful and meaningful name....
401pm Ji. Today just I got sadhak sanjivani Gita of Gita press...
Thank you so much.

129pm 11/10/2018
Ji today I got two copies of B. Geeta Sanjivani....... Thank you very very very much..... YOU r really great..... I am really thankful to you...

335pm 14/10/2018
Wishing a most auspicious Chandi Homa and blissful Navaratri. Jai Gurudev
342pm Harih Om! Very thankful for sending me the Chandi homa wishes:) he introduced parayana of Devi mahatmyam. Wish you happy Navaratri. Swami's daughter

634am 19/10/2018 Dussehra
Jai Gurudev Swamiji. Vijay Dashami greetings = victory over 10 senses and organs of action = overcoming toxins, distractions and veil with Guru Grace.
858am
Jai Gurudev
Jai Maa
Let the Divine Grace of Gurudev and Jagatjanani Maa Durga Guide and Protect our Spiritual and Secular life. May we abide in Thee for ever.

1242pm 20/10/2018
Congratulations! Your new Sim no <> has been activated for you're A-Mobile <>.
249pm 21/10/2018
Update: SMS service has been started for A-mobile. You can continue using the service.

1214pm 22/10/2018
Mummy Darling thy birthday glows radiates and fills all with charm
121pm It reflects love of my near n dear ones

917pm 23/10/2018
Radha today it is Sharad Poornima. Please see the beautiful moon reflecting your glory
105pm 24/10/2018 Here we celebrate today.... Happy Sharad Poornima... My Diksha day
109pm Ooo Devi...thee are richly blessed and full of Divinity. Happiness Strength and Auspiciousness at your holy feet.
424pm ji my diksha day was Thursday 7th October 1999. Which date is yours Radha?
504pm My date which is second Brahmachari Diksha is 25-10-2007. Also First Mantra diksha date is in 1999. Not remembering date...
636pm Devi chand nikal aaya. Please please go and see. The rays make eyes healthy and joints become strong
657pm Lekin yha se nhi dikhta
713pm ji aap niche jaana ya phir terrace par. Sharad Poornima ko Sri Krishna gopiyon ke saath raas leela chand ki kirano ke dwara aap mein bhar dete hain
853pm Terrace par ja ke aayi... Moon bhaut sundar hai.. Thanks
748am 25/10/2018 yeh hui na baat. Aapne krishna ka dil jeet liya. I am proud of you. Aap pe gurumaa ki apar kripa. Aap Nachiketas ki tarah uttam adhikari hain.

445pm 27/10/2018 Karva Chauth
Tripura Sundari talked for 90 minutes. She warmed up and displayed grit regarding her new HP laptop switched on for first time.

755pm 2/11/2018
Yashoda called. Fully at ease in the Lord. Living a peaceful, cheerful life.

847am 5/11/2018
Wishes for a purifying Dhanteras n Diwali that strengthens Sattva
and bestows an effulgent aura of Divine. 848am Jai Gurudev
Many thanks Ashwini!! Wishing you all happy Dhanteras too... Bless
you 🖤 soothing rain

842am 5/11/2018
Jai Gurudev Swamiji. Wishes for a purifying Dhanteras n Diwali that
banishes all doubts
946am Ashwani ji Maharaj ki Jai ho. Hope everything is Fine with
you. May Bliss Peace and Happiness be your constant Companion.
Keep Praying Keep Smiling Keep Dancing but keep sending sms
too . Ha ha ha Om Thy Own Self
956am Swamiji, you express so well. Reading your sms gives me so
much purity and a sense of that the Divine is with me
10am Yes Not only the Divine is With us, we are Divinity
Personification, Tiger ke Bache to Tiger hi honge na! Let's
remember our real nature and enjoy life with a S M I L E

130pm 11/11/2018
Thick scent as Air hugged me and we melded and became one.
Time stopped as oblivious to all on the main road we were.

1245pm 16/11/2018
No no I'm progressing. That one class was enough to get going. I'll
share my chanting in a few days. RajW
103pm Thanks dear. All the very best.

826am 17/11/2018
Morning Uncle. Sat Sri Akal ji. Happy Gurpurab
916am Thank you 🖤......Same to you Ji......... Have a blissful day

708pm 19/11/2018
Aaje Tulsi Vivah ni Khub Vadhai Ho! Hari Om, Jay Bhagwan. Divya
swarup

744pm 19/11/2018
Dear Monty, Jai Sri Gurudev ji, really brave of you to take the step you have taken 2wards your Spiritual goal. With admiring Holistic regards. Please stay in touch. Surpal from Norway.

826pm 22/11/2018
Wah Mont Sri, as ever, got the much-needed upliftment, in your few words.
933 pm All your grace and purity Jee

1244pm 24/11/2018
Papa i am having an astonishing experience and a most wonderful course.
222pm That's great news plus being with GuruDev all these days is the best part.

113pm 24/11/2018
having an extraordinary Gurpurab with Vigyan Bhairav - the Self Realization techniques of Kashmir Shaivism - at the feet of Guruji

616pm 25/11/2018
Vigyan Bhairav Shivir mein adbhut anubhav. Jai Shri Krishna.

808pm 26/11/2018 from flight
Please do not feel sorry. i am fine and grateful. thankyou ji for calling. All the Best.

155pm 29/11/2018
Wish you happy journey... Sorry for trouble... Take care
157pm Thank you Radha. Please be happy ji. Prayers for your well-being, Safety and Strength. Take care

757pm 29/11/2018 I'm sure you are correct.
But we too are responsible for our circumstances to a great extent. Let's make our choices better for self and divine. Arunachal.
759pm Yes Yes Yes. The Truth clearly manifests for a Karma Yogi.

616pm 11/12/2018
Dear will reach home early morning 3am. Hope gate will be open.
706pm Yes dear Take my name.

818pm 12/12/2018
oṃ dyau: śāntir antarikṣa gum śānti: pṛthvī śāntir āpa: śāntir
oṣadhaya: śānti:

vanaspataya: śāntir viśve devā: śāntir brahma śānti: sarvam̐ śānti:
śāntir eva śānti: sā mā śāntir edhi

oṃ śānti: śānti: śānti:
837pm 🤍 Thank you so much Ashwini Bhaiya.

6pm 15/12/2018
Devi called at 6pm. Then we chatted happily at 747pm.
915pm Good night ji. Sleep tight

1001am 18/12/2018
Reached Mummyji. Thanks for your love
503pm Missing you..had good times take care see you on Saturday

1011am 18/12/2018
Pranaams Mataji. Such a calm serene Bhagavad Gita Jayanti. Jai
Gurudev.
1121am Yes Ashwini all love and blessings

1135am 20/12/2018
ji main Bombay ja raha hun and train halts there. Remembered.
1139am Kaise? Baby was tickled and chatted happily.

112am 22/12/2018
train has halted. Thee are too far. Okay no prob.

Mummyji enjoying a calm drive.
856pm 24/12/2018 Ok...missing you

25/12/2018. Gyaneshwari received

107pm 25/12/2018
Bhaiya, we are already missing you soo much :)
109pm Princess am just enjoying a simple drive thru marine drive
and all the famous places with my nephew. Be with thee soon...
310pm Ohh wow! Marine drive...enjoiiii bhaiya :):)

359pm 27/12/2018
Reached home. Thanks very much Princess
5pm Ohh nice...it was sooo much fun...come again Bhaiya, and
come soooon :)

401pm 27/12/2018
Reached home. Thanks very much Dvika. Monty
407pm No problem Tauji! Take care

1111pm 29/12/2018
Birthdays are triggers for exponential growth...jai gurudev.
309pm 30/12/2018 Exactly! Thanks Ashwani! Jai Gurudev!!! AnujS

1008am 31/12/2018
koti koti pranaam. happy new year.
1020am Wish you Happy New Year

1157am 1/12/2018 Jai Gurudev!!
So happy to receives your warm message...Only love and blessings
flow whenever I think of you...May God shower HIS Kindest
blessings on you always!! Happy New Year 2019. Limitnbound

602am 2/12/2018

Mont Sri, thee are blessed to have presented the essence of Geeta. I read many parts of it. It's exact....

618am Jee aap dhanya hain. Aap ko milne ke baad meri life khil paayi hai.

Attraction

621am 16/4/2018
a blissful somvar amavasya
1351pm Happy somvati amavasya. Be loved

935pm 17/4/2018
Lord met me in Train varanasi rail yatra said Satyavati at 10am on 28/2/2018

749pm 24/4/2018
She made contact

320pm 25/4/2018
Please look at the karaka notes and let me know.. Also please send me PDF file of prathmavritti. I have only first part.

7pm 25/4/2018
KDpika and family made it all come together so easily at Rudra Puja and Havan

1030pm 25/4/2018
After Rudra Puja, L and his parents met in Dukh Niwaran Saab for a quaint proposal. A new beginning.

1104am 26/4/2018
Sundari called and said sweetly - you called why?
942am Yes I got it. But I don't know how to download it. Please
258pm Devi have sent Chap 4-8. You said you have 1st book so do you need Chap 1-3 also? Please tell
307pm Yes It's OK
308pm achha ji achha

6pm 26/4/2018 Dera Bassi
HKaur team from Panchkula Mohali Chandigarh organised Rudra
Puja with grace showering on all, with Agnihotra at 6:53:17pm

932am 27/4/2018
Darling called and chatted happily

828am 28/4/2018
happy Buddha Poornima. a wisdom filled life
949am Thank you dear Bhaiya :) With Love , smiles and regards
from me and d :)
1002am Thank you soo much Bhaiya for your valuable blessings
showered.... Jai Guru Dev. Jaipur
1205pm a calm wise and benign Buddha Poornima. Ashwini
1221pm Om . Om. Om. Same warm wishes to you all.... How is the
Rudra saadhanaa proceeding? Sai
1232pm ji we are having Rudra Puja Satsang twice a month and
three sets of devotees are there - some for wisdom some for
Sanskrit Grammar and some for Chanting
1237pm Whatever the reason, as long as the bees are attracted to
honey, it's ok
1313pm my sundari replied - Yes. Thanks for help

1140am 28/4/2018
At plot site, cool breeze even at peak of noon. tiling expected to be
over next week. Repair resurfacing of main highway in front of
colony also in progress.
1147am Great Papa. work will progress speedily now

751am 29/4/2018
Devi called and chatted happily inviting me. And said with a touch
of anger - unse bahut prem aa raha hai – my playful response - O
she loves me dearly.
808am Thank you Devi for calling. I am feeling very happy ji

1133am 7/5/2018 Monday
At 1115am Lord met with unparalleled belongingness and on being
offered the book, glanced keenly and said "Maheshwar Sutras" and
nodded his head with a Yes! (Go on with Sanskrit work…)
Badrivishala after Rudra Puja.

110pm
Pranaams Mataji, couldn't get travel confirmation so will visit
another time. Jai Gurudev ashwini
156pm Ok. All love and best wishes

1126am 8/5/2018
called honey and she said sweetly "Maine abhi yaad hi kiya aur
aapki call aa gayi".

12noon 9/5/2018
pleased bharya calls to say daughter's joining new job and finance
is going well

928pm 9/5/2018
excited bharya says daughter will join PhD at UK.

1030am 10/5/2018
babyBeauty calls to say she heard Guruji's voice for the first time as
Swatantaranand called Guruji and put it on speakerphone for her!!!
the conversation was something to do with Australia visit and also
Swatantaranand's going to Bangalore for Tera May.

Dewdrop had been invited by Swatantaranand for diksha.

1012am 11/5/2018
Defiant said angrily with a touch of passion - if train is not available
i will stay till 16th and go with you…

825pm 11/5/2018
I am going for Leh advance Course with Rishi ji from 10/6 to 17/6
Also I am going for Kailash Mansarovar AMP with Rishi ji from 21/8
to 31/8. We will be taking dip in Mansarovar lake on Sharavan
Purnima! AnujS
914pm wonderful. that is strengthening purifying elevating

923am 13/5/2018
Harih Om! My pranams to Guruji on this special today
928am Dear Swami daughter, many thanks. Wish you love and
blessings of Divine

940am 13/5/2018 Sunday
It's the day the wave remembers the ocean from which it was born.
Happy Tera May
941am Woww...Bhaiya you have said it all and so so so
beautifully...love and regards...

129pm
wow. all of us meditated together. Our Lord loves us too much
141pm Bhaiya it always feels so nice after talking to you. Thank you
for being a part of our life. JGD 🖤 Consort

14/5/2018 730am to 9am Durga Homa
Offering with Durga Suktam mantras.
Lord came around 9am, then Rudra Puja. a terrible time of wanting
to escape from apparent clutches of A Ashram stories...And of Sai
Ved Sat story later in afternoon.
Bhaiya the day began with Innova drop by Radha to Yagnashala.
Ended with plans for Goshala in Chidambaram and smooth ride to
station. Thankyou Thankyou Thankyou. Jai Gurudev.

324pm 15/5/2018 Amavasya
ji aap pahunch gayi? Jay Ho!
429pm Ha ji me phonch gai hun.. Bhaut achha mausam hai yahan..
Bilkul thanda

354pm 17/5/2018
Devi aapne email dekhi?
440pm Abhi nhi dekhi. Yahan network weak hai. Main bhaut dense forest me hun abhi.
530pm accha! agar sher ya bhalu mile to meri taraf se bhi namastey kahna...

1141am 18/5/2018
Devi email padhne ke liye shukriya.
1152am ji! Got your mail... It's good. Thank you so much..
109pm Sorry for late reply
202pm ji koi baat nahin. i am happy that you are in a cool safe place in the lap of mother nature.

639pm 19/5/2018
Tripura Sundari aapki sadhana siddh ho aur aap Lotus ke saman bright - beautiful - benevolent ban jayen

1229pm 22/5/2018 (got a strong pull)
Devi kya aapne yaad kiya?
1237pm Roj krti hun. Koi nyi bat nhi

9pm 24/5/2018
Yes bhaiya I received bhasma . Thank you very much. Grateful to you. Coolness

622am 26/5/2018
Good Morning Devi. Ji Poornima aa rahi hai...aapne chaand ko dekha?
727am Hann. Very good morning....Aaj baat karenge 11 bje baad...
1209 she called and said, i will stay with you in Rishikesh and take me to Joshi Math...spoke for 13 min

935pm 31/5/2018
Dearie spoke softly

111pm 2/6/2018
Satyavati called from Lord's Darshan line
5-7pm Rudra Puja at Maur Mandi
935pm a happy Satyavati called describing a sanyam when Lord
took yogasana session and on 19th May ignited in VM.

936pm Dearie called. Regarding Aswarup lectures DVD

1217pm 4/6/2018
yes i think. please try and call if you need help.
1307pm Don't worry. Whenever I will try, will ask your help. Today
some program is there so I am busy.

714pm 10/6/2018
from Kathgodam Baby called and said i am in train. please come to
pick me.

428am Monday 11/6/2018 Dwadashi
Darshan of Beloved

756am 11/6/2018
Honey called during Havan Purnahuti at Sanatan Mandir adjacent
St. Anne School Dehradun. aap kahan hain? come! she commanded.

10am Lord she spoke just as thee. Mooladhar Chakra opens up with
Ganesha smaran who removes Vighna.

8:30pm 11/6/2018 after Rudra Puja and Ganga Aarti
Sundari said in swami dining room DAshram, "i came to see you,
you were eating but you didn't even look at me". She pouted, "so i
left in a hurry".

12/6/2018
1:15pm dew drop gave the sweetest khoya made by her love and
said - eat all of this you alone only…

838am 13/6/2018
W gave aashirvad. Very Happy

16:19 pm 17/6/2018
11th June is the day when after handing over my darling safely to her path, the Lord stepped in and said 'you shall always be protected. you shall always be well taken care of'.
17th June after morning Yoga, after a rain that lasted 5 hours when Nature became all joyous, when the weather became perfect, my being left. i felt like a log of wood. i experienced a total stillness. Then beloved called and poured her heart out. She spoke for 23 minutes. in her soft silken voice. she showered love. then she was gone with a finality.

Beginning

A new beginning awaits. A new life without fear beckons. Take it my friend. Walk unhurriedly. walk Tall. it is a homecoming. it is a fresh start. welcome to a fabulous journey. Jai Gurudev. 16:31pm

- Earlier at 7:15 Jee called while in Yoga class.

- Maiden's email seen at noon, after uploading Patanjali to my heart's content, coming to her as she opened up and we chatted in glee.

The path to freedom is always simple and straight.

633pm 21/6/2018
Baby Beauty spoke for 9 min, pausing frequently and whispering - i love you lord - in each pause.

809am 24/6/2018
Most Divine Goddess. Felicitations and Jubilations on your Happy Birthday. May you radiate Beauty and spread Joy. koti koti pranaam.
1042am ji ek khush khabari. Aapki yaad aayi aur maine badiya bhojan liya. Thank you ji
1232pm Thank you so much prabhu

12pm 24/6/2018
Dear Bhaiyya, we will have a look. We remember you, the Vasad trip and your words, "Yeh prasadam kismet walon ko milta hai!" for the Ashram food. Do drop down to Ahmedabad someday. Warm regards AbNid
1201pm Thanks very much. ok will visit soon.

1244pm
Dear Ashwini ji
It is indeed a pleasure to know about publication of your hard work in the form of book. Congratulations and well wishes for this. I am placing order for the same with a promise whenever we meet you will give your autograph on the book. Love Vivek
1311pm Yes what a divine reply. Grateful Pranaams.

904am 26/6/2018
Hello Ashwini, received another Gift from you ;). Will read someday. Keep doing good work. DP
957am Sure. swami ji, and congratulations for writing this book ♥ Regards n Jgd. Infatuated.

406pm 28/6/2018
Ji, Got your Courier of Patanjali Yoga book. Thanks
913pm Devi aapne khush kar diya. Thanks shukriya dhanyavad.
Happy Poornima.

631am 30 June 2018
Wishing you a very happy birthday dear Bhai. May God bless you
with health and happiness to continue the seva that you are doing.

823am Sshank from Bilaspur Gurukul called happily

1021am
Many Happy Returns of the day. May you have a wonderful and
Blessed Year ahead. Monica
1027am grateful Thanks beloved Monica

336pm Wishing you many many happy returns of the day dear
Ashwini bhai....
338pm wow Som. It's a wonderful and truly great wish

1014pm
Jgd Mamu, wish you happy bday. L

825pm 1/7/2018
Finished reading your book sometime back. Most of it went beyond
my comprehension. Some things sank into the subconscious. I
could comprehend just a small part. While reading I remembered
Atlas Shrugged.
829pm wow. add this line too in the Review.

1115am 2/7/2018
Dera Ashwini
Received your book today. Seems to be a good one, full of content.
Let me go through it than I will talk to you. Reminding you of the
autograph....
1121am Most Respected Vivek ji. That is a great honor from yourself.
Thanks so much. Autograph is sure

208pm 3/7/2018
Ashwini ji. jai gurudev. my daughter got admission at St. Stephens
college Delhi university for BA Hons Economics course. We are
relocating to Delhi on 10th july. Will definitely buy the books, read
them and get back to you. With warm regards. V-san

1045am 4/7/2018
Consort and her Mum talked for an hour relating Guruji's grace and
recounting miracles and made me feel strong and fearless.

1029pm 4/7/2018
Namaste ji. Great news and congratulations. I'll see the book.
Earlier sent msg failed, and call too didn't go thru. Good luck for
any future project(s). V

952am 8/7/2018
Devi how are you ji? Happy and enjoying pleasant weather...
1211pm Good morning… I am fine...

1115am 12/7/2018
i spent one day in Nagpur Gurukul and one day in Bilaspur. Pushpa
remembers you very much.
447pm Wow good.. Have a nice time...

410pm 20/7/2018
she called 434pm and spoke for 28min in glee

247pm 23/7/2018

Namaste!

I acknowledge with great thanks receipt of your beautiful book DHATUPATHA - Verbs in 5 Lakaras received through courier.

The book is very well presented . The copy is kept for our Library. I will review. Thank you once again. Jai Gurudev

238pm Jai Gurudev. Most grateful pranaams

327pm 23/7/2018

Mont Sri, I've uploaded Japji Sahib PDF after best I could do on oboroi

328pm Wonderful. Jee that will become a revered and sought for edition

1210pm 24/7/2018

Baby Beauty called, spoke for 11min

735am 27/7/2018

Jay Bhagvan Guru Purnimani subhecha sah Namonarayan. Aatma marge Khub pragati Thay aevi guru charanma prarthna. Divya swarup

1024am Many Thanks. A day of going inwards. Deep relaxation and Peace. Jay Bhagawan

1043am Muni Maharaj ji aajse ek salka moun karnevale he abhi vahelal se bhavnagar ja rahe he. Bat karni ho to kar sakte ho

1103am Muni Maharaj happily gave blessings and asked for new book.

926am Guru Poornima

Happy Gurupurnima. Jai Gurudev.

1021am Thank you Govindji. A fine day of relaxation

1:30pm Ji Maa ko koti koti pranaam. Aapke Mummy Papa ke bhi charan sparsh.
444pm Function is done. Going to home. Today is grahan..

2pm 27/7/2017 Guru Poornima
Rudrabhisheka at new home

353pm 27/7/2018
Hari Om, be with Guru, be like Guru. Yashoda
4pm Yashoda chatted happily for 20min
451pm Consort chatted nicely for 5min

1134am 31/7/2018 Smandir called joyfully, said Nanu got admission in DU.

1009pm 10/8/2018
Ji . Got the ghee and Rudra pooja small book parcel... Thanks a lot.
1010pm Welcome Devi

2:25pm 11/8/2018 Amavasya
Dear Ash.... glad to inform that son received the approval email from CEmbassy yesterday. Travelling to Kolkata now for submitting passport at Kolkata vfs... thanks so much for all the good wishes and blessings for son...
304pm wow wow wow. All the very best for a smooth journey abroad and a high-class education

219pm 13/8/2018 Shravan Rudra Puja
Dear Muni Maharaj ji, Jay Bhagawan. Today blue dart courier will give my book parcel to you. Ashwini
227pm OK

856pm A beautiful, enlivening and aspiration fulfilling Shravan Rudra Puja.

859pm Thank you so much Ashwini!! God bless you and everyone at home. bharya cool rain showers

916pm Hari Om Anirudh

901pm Got the yoga book today. Thank you so much

901pm koti koti pranaams Devi

0014am 14/8/2018

Aaj sham ko dono kitabe mil gai. Aapne bhaut hi sundar karya kiya hai. HARIOM. Muni Maharaj

657am Dhanyawad. Koti koti pranaam. Jay Bhagwan

738am 15/8/2018

Wish you happy journey.. All the best for your course.

1045am Thank you Devi. You are very caring ji. Apna khyal Rakhna.

335pm 18/8/2018

Today I got karmakand bhaskar book from gayatri parivar… Thank you so much

405pm Devi hope you like it ji.

557pm Yes its nice book.. How is the ashram schedule? Is everything comfortable? Feeling good??

645pm Yes ji. Feeling very good. Room is comfortable.

Dinacharya

653pm 18/8/2018

1 Morning Meditation 5 to 6am.

2 Breakfast 7am.

3 Patanjali Yoga Sutras 7:30 to 8:15 am.

4 Upanishad class 8:20 to 9:05am.

5 Narad Bhakti Sutras 9:10 to 9:55am.

6 Philosophy class 10 to 10:45am.

7 Lunch 11am

8 Bhagavad Gita 3:15 to 4pm.

9 Cleaning seva 4:15 to 4:45pm.

10 Yoga class 5 to 6:15pm.

11 Dinner 7pm.

655pm
Ohhhh it's too hectic.... Take care..

1041am 19/8/2018
Wish you a great course and a wonderful darshan
136pm Thank you. Had darshan today after he came out of
yagnashala after anandutsav session. Git

742pm 19/8/2018
Radha aapko somvar Rudra Puja ka hardik abhivadan.
235pm 20/8/2018 Thanks
244pm ji how was your Puja???
840pm It was nice

129pm 22/8/2018
All the very best to Sdha for a befitting union.
132pm She would be delighted to get your blessings. Arr

1036pm 23/8/2018
Received manual of spine care program today and had very good
darshan of gurudev and pics too with him, thanks for your support
for this ttp.....it was a very enriching experience....
333am 24/8/2018 Excellent. It will benefit many participants across
Punjab and beyond.

1137am 24/8/2018 Pradosh
Tripura Sundari you did magic. With your blessings i got very tasty
lunch. Matar paneer, yellow dal and lots of kheer

959pm 24/8/2018
Met guruji today also. Git
333am 25/8/2018 Wonderful. Did He say something?
836am Just passed by.... gave a letter and a flower
122pm That's a supreme blessing. His presence'll alwaysbewith you

931am 25/8/2018
We are on our way to Delhi to see off son at the airport. He is flying
abroad tomorrow.
1208pm Yippee. That is the big moment. All grace be with him. Jai
Gurudev. Om Shanti

126pm 25/8/2018 Saturday
On Friday we went inside badrivishala and didi arranged our
meeting with Him so he blessed our manuals and we took pics with
him...i'm standing next to Him.
127pm Excellent. All the best for great courses and a superb life

636am 26/8/2018 Paurnami
Happy Raksha Bandhan Bhai.
1004am thank you very much. a Shravan Poornima with rains is a
profound blessing

1248pm
Happy Rakshabandhan.
1250pm Tripura Sundari bahut bahut dhanyavad. Koti koti
pranaam. ji wish you presence and darshan of Bhagvan Shiv.

A joyous Rakhi and a fulfilling Shravan Poornima.

Devi today it is World Sanskrit Day.

530pm Got Rakhi tied by a Punjabi.
545pm Rakhi by a saintly lady.
6pm Yagyopavit in Samadhi Mandir
645pm 3rd Rakhi by the German.
902pm Happy rakshabandhan dear Bhaiya :):)
607am 27/8/2018 Divine Princess, it is such a great fortune to
celebrate a happy Rakshabandhan day. Thank you very much.

Book Review

1151pm 27/2/2018
Jai Gurudev Ashwiniji,

I hope you get this message.

I have been learning Rudram chanting for many years (or trying to, at least), and recently came across your wonderful online book shop. You can only imagine my excitement at finding this treasure trove of knowledge. I had just been at the point where my chanting of Namakam and Chamakam was flowing better, and I wanted to learn more about the before-and-after verses for the puja specifically as performed at Bangalore ashram. I was a bit shocked to find your book at all, since for years I had been piecing together verses from the internet, and matching them with the puja recording on youtube (the big one from Navratri at ashram)

I had a question about the online store (US) - under the title 'Rudra Puja : Simple, Complete, Profound (Sanskrit)', there are two separate books that look similar, except one is more expensive and has a nicer-looking cover. I bought the one with the simple cover that was $14. I was wondering if the other one that is $17+ is the same book, or if there is any different content in there.

Also, I am just starting to read and learn the Sankalpa part for the first time. Would you mind if I asked you some questions about the process of including the names/places/time/etc.?

Thanks so much-Pawan P

948am 2/9/2018

Om namo narayanaaya, best wishes for sri krishna janmashtami, may bhagavan bless you and family in all respects. Sri kailas ashram rishikesh.

1139pm 2/9/2018

ji today i saw in DAshram Temple - Hemvati samet Sri Gangadhareshwar

145pm 3/9/2018

Namaste Ashwini ji
Happy Sri Krishna JANMASTHAMI and Greetings of the season. Jai Gurudev.
648pm Jai Gurudev ji. Strong pull of Divine Brahman and absorption in deep Samadhi. Happy Janmashtami

1248pm 5/9/2018

Wishing you a very Happy Teacher's Day.... you make an ideal teacher, who teaches by being an "example" to follow.... you really inspire my friend, my brother....my teacher...!! ♥
302pm Dearest Som, it is mutual that we learn from each other and thereby reflect his glory. Wish you a divine Teacher's Day

652pm 5/9/2018

Happy teachers day...when r u coming home? with love and best wishes
746pm Hopefully around Diwali

828pm 7/9/2018

Radha ki jai. A very beautiful happy joyous Radha Ashtami
941pm Achha...

722am 21/9/2018

Good morning...keep enjoying each breath...with love

205pm Mummy can i come in mid Dec? Are you available?

217pm Available before mid-Dec. Say till Dec 17 18

410pm Wow wonderful. Hope to spend 10th to 18th at thy feet

439pm Great. looking forward dear to have you with us.

8th is the Day

When Lord visited

this day the 8th of April my mood was dull and my spirits were low
and i was up against the wall.

it was a day of talking to myself. of seeing if i could communicate
and express. it was also a moment of refreshing the priority. i asked
"what do i do? what is it that i want to spend my time and talents
on? how do i exist and what is important?

since there was a dullness and a dryness and a drain of the faculties,
no suitable answer presented itself. the mind condensed and
became unresponsive. the limbs felt listless.

then a prayer burst forth. i simply told Guruji that i needed help. i
told him that i wanted his support. i said i was at a loss.

it was slow in unfurling. like the time it takes for a rose bud to open.
it takes an endless hour. but it happened. the Lord himself visited.

the energy began to flow, the faculties started to function and the
clouds passed away. consciousness swelled up and became bright.
i laughed.

life was again rosy and smiling.

once the inner space clears, the sunlight filters through and life is
whole again. 903am 12/4/2018

28/4/2018

when rajas rises you can't keep still. that is why they invented the smartphone. to keep all senses engaged and excited.

before an event a cloud might arise. that is hazy or dull or a put down.

after the event Time works its magic. after a while it wipes the mind clean of the event and its residue.

Jai Gurudev 840pm

Enlightenment

Gurudev says

Enlightenment is becoming a child again. Uncomplicated. Enlightenment is returning to simplicity. It is the faith that Truth will Triumph.

Sojourn Sept 2015

janmashtami Delhi
navaratri bangalore ashram
diwali pilani ranchi chhath

PNR:2409373570,TRAIN:14712,
DOJ:09-09-15,CC, Wednesday
PTA-HW,Dep:09:05, ,C2 60,
Fare:345,SC:45.6+PG CHGS

PNR:2109373296,TRAIN:12018,
DOJ:12-09-15,1A, Saturday
HW-NDLS,Dep:18:15, ,RLWL 5,
Fare:1270,SC:45.6+PG CHGS

Bangalore Rajdhani
PNR:2752508398, TRAIN:22692,
DOJ:07-10-15,3A, Wednesday
NGP-SBC,Dep:N.A., 10am, RLWL 6,
Fare:2030,SC:45.6+PG CHGS
dep 1025am arr 0640am

PNR:4211155833,TRAIN:22691,
DOJ:25-10-15,3A, Sunday
SBC-NGP,Dep:N.A., 8pm , Confirmed
Fare:2070,SC:45.6+PG CHGS
dep 2020pm arr 1525pm

Sep 5, 2015

What is deatH?

The feeling or emotion of separating. the moment of going away.
the time when one departs.

Death is too short. Only lasts a few minutes or an hour. Soon one is
on one's way. Then the moment has passed. The death has been
forgotten.

What is Between Death and Life?
simply a journey akin to a bus boat plane or train ride if one is alone
and thoughts are sticky.

Sticky as in perplexed agitated strung. a journey when one is
looking at the clock. Wondering when will the destination arrive.
when shall it end?

to reiterate. Death is simply a point of separation. Death to Life is
simply a few hours journey, that might stretch to half a day or bit
more.

what is it all About? what is the Purpose? just to become distilled.
just to come unstuck असंगोऽहम् ।
Distilled from what? Unstuck from what?

the baggage. the wrapping. the luggage that had been given to
keep one infatuated. the packaging on oneself to pass the time in
transit.

One simply gets a trajectory from the pool of stillness to experience motion or emotion. Then after a few cycles where one builds on the luggage and wrapping if a longer game is desired, it gets prolonged.

No big deal. Just a play. Just some toying that one grows out of or gets tired of. Then back to the pool.

Jai Gurudev 14:28pm 12/7/2018 Bilaspur to Ranchi superfast.

The False and weaK

6th Aug 2015 Shravan Saptami

i pondered long and hard.
i struggled to face myself.

i asked what was the falsehood.
What was the weakness in me.

In my life which were the undesirable moments?
what was it that needed to be avoided, improved, adjusted or
retuned?

it wasn't easy.
took a while figuring it out.
unraveling the thoughts, desires, temptations.
unconnecting the habits, notions, opinions, patterns.

the thoughts and the logical conclusions and the comforts,
pleasures, and "i'm used to this", "i prefer this" such programs,
loops, routines
were many.

these needed to be separated, or kept at bay, at least for a while.

then in bits bit by bit, somethings became apparent (or so i think).

it is alright.
everything is okay.

Yep. Yes. Yeah.

it is all desirable.
it is all welcome.
it is all correct.

Yes. Yeah. Yep.

Om Namah Shivaya.
ॐ नमः शीवाय ।
Om = the creation = the creator
Na = Earth
Ma = Water
Shi = Fire
Va = Air
Ya = Space

i.e. The Lord and His tools. His Resources. Men. Machines.

i.e. He

got it...?
certainly not.

ok well, everything and anything and something, it is nothing but
He. The Lord.

got it...?
are you kidding? i'm blank.

ok. let us try another tack.

all weaknesses and strengths,
all fears and falsehoods or
tranquility and truths.
all projects all works all events all expressions all moments.
all edifices all roles
all laws all broken laws all promises broken unbroken.
all rules all rulers.

all.

Just He. His Will. His direction. His path. Him.

Jai Gurudev.
1638pm
onboard indigo flight baroda to delhi.

Chitra Gupt

The Form hidden (impressions deep).

perhaps we have heard this term.

i heard it some time ago in my gurukul.

and also saw about it in a Mahabharata episode on epic channel.

Lord Yama. familiar to all of us as TIME.
as the watch on our wrist.
as the clock on the bedroom wall.
as the alarm in my Moto E.
as the led digits on my smartphone.

or as some other principle.

and then it was said...heard...
that
"there is an accounting.
a recording.
of all my thoughts. words. actions."
"perhaps feelings and sensations too."

today while sitting in the Shankaracharya Sharda Math at the
Dwarka Temple in Gujarat,
this.
such notions.
these statements.

(about the recordings),
It flashed thus:-

friend
there is no external record.
there is no google nor facebook to record and keep conversations.
or emails.
or flings.

That the only record keeper is me.
And, my accounting is moody seasonal eventual.
sometimes i record, other times i don't.
my recording is discontinuous, haphazard, willful.

many times i record yet do not remember. sometimes i do not
record yet it is revealed.

over a long period of time, i get distilled and transparent
at that time if i notice my accounts, i wish to undergo a tapasya. a
frugal lifestyle.

and the Lord happily grants me.

That's about it.

Jai Gurudev.
2316pm Shravan Monday. 3 Aug 2015. Dwarka Temple Town. by the
Arabian sea. by the gentle lapping waves. by the silvery waters that
caught the sun or the moon.

Meditation 18.7.2015 Alipurduar

Mind Body Soul
3 circles 3 distinct components

the mechanics of mind and of body are largely known to you i assume.

i am letting out a prime secret.
the soul only craves for meditation. it only desires for meditation.
the soul wishes and prays that it may get meditation.

Math
$1+1 = 2$ body mechanics
$1-1 = 0$ mind mechanics
----------- soul
$1 \times 1 = 1$
$1/1 = 1$
$1^1 = 1$
$^/1 = 1$
----
body works by proper food and lots of exercise
go inwards
mind works by good rest and some space and freedom
dive a bit deeper
soul works only by meditation
----
and the world of the soul is multidimensional, infinite planes
whereas the body is a 3D entity
mind is a space time entity i.e. 4D

Notes

Happiness is right here and now.
Joyful and Responsible living is available to all. Thru Meditation.

Meditation improves our mind and brings more happiness.

Similarly the Practice of Meditation shifts our craving for drugs
towards proper nourishing food, and hey presto one is off drugs in
no time. what does Meditation do? Simply it uncovers our inborn
talents and unites one's mind and body towards achieving that.

Meditation directly aligns our mind and body towards what is good
for it. Meditation uncovers our godly talents and rekindles our
hobbies. thus we forget our need for drugs.

After all, what is addiction? Let us take a closer look.
Any long-term habit that proves to be detrimental to one's health
and that drains our pocket. Any interest that destroys our
judgement and makes us dependent on money. Any passion that
proves to be harmful to our fellow beings and society.

Now who drives such an interest? The society around us. The
company we keep. The big advertisements for liquor and smoking.
The peer pressure at workplace or at a professional college. The
huge dependence on allopathy medications.

If we can handle this and regulate it, drug usage will drop in no time.
This is YOUR task.

We are available simply to guide. To the preventive mechanism and to the curing mechanism.

You are the law makers and enforcers, so this role is yours.
Jai Gurudev

Finding Peace

i found my peace in Hem. thru Him fell grace and drenched me.

i found my peace in Intimate, thru Him his profoundness got glimpsed.

i found my peace in Just, as my other body the Lord revealed.

and in Git and in Chhot and in W n M n J.

how come it came? how come peace came?

how can peace come? how can it come? it is all happening ain't enough. something more is to be done. what is it what is that.

Go back to the beginning and define peace. a blend of environment weather situations events for the clueless. and something within for the saint.

can i will away misery misfortune and mistake? yes certainly for myself i can. maybe for another i redefine the sounds and then it seems for another as well.

for each the pattern is slightly offset, relatively abounds in great measure and each sound has another connotation. such is termed loosely as Hukum. as Order. as Natural Law, as the Creator's Will.

Loosely for some talk about Free Will. Actually bound will and free will are the same sounds. And nature, preferring diversity in its waking state, gave more than one word to the same thing.

Even though in a smaller circle yes and no, night and day, boy or girl are two words, the bigger circle comfortably houses both and so the words mean the same there.

1012am Dwadashi 29 June. Chandigarh.

And again the reel starts and the drama unfolds. all actors and
emotions get portrayed, anything and sundry gets expressed.

some say hold, others say continue, few say rewind, fast forward,
all demands appear.

is it true only one demand gets satisfied? is it true only some desire
gets fulfilled?

True and untrue both. how come?
relativity is one possible answer. what is true from an angle
becomes false from another until one realizes both true and false
and in-between mean the same from yet another perspective.

so then what? dunno.
sail on, flow as you wish or as your circumstances dictate. and
someday the Lord will catch you.

will He? that is certain. history says so. so do our parents. so does
the news and the dreams too.

What if it ain't timely...
give Him a break, let Him free to do as He pleases.

then what do the scriptures says. what do the temples say. what do
the saints say. what do the schools say?.

just hang on. hold on to one thing something that catches your fancy and nourish it. also feed the hungry once in a while. nurture nature sometimes. somethings forgive and forget. come what may pursue your dream. live such that pleases you.

June 29, 2015

Epilogue

Nature and Emotions are in a flux.

Someday grace intervenes, and you melt away.

सर्वे भवन्तु सुखिनः । सर्वे सन्तु निरामयाः ।

सर्वे भद्राणि पश्यन्तु । मा कश्चिद् दुःख भाग्भवेत् ॥

ॐ शान्तिः शान्तिः शान्तिः ॥

When faith has blossomed in life,
Every step is led by the Divine.

Sri Sri Ravi Shankar

Om Namah Shivaya

जय गुरुदेव